Yorkshire Coastline

River Tees to Bridlington.

Ian Smith

SANDHILL PRESS

My thanks go to all who have helped, by encouragement, by sharing my walks, by sharing their knowledge.

To E

The section maps are to a scale of about 1:45000, and are based upon the 1985 Ordnance Survey Landranger 1:50 000 maps with the permission of the Controller of Her Majesty's Stationery Office © Crown Copyright.

First published in Great Britain by Sandhill Press Limited, 17 Castle Street, Warkworth, MORPETH, Northumberland, NE65 OUW, 1990

Copyright © Ian Smith 1989.

ISBN 0 946098 17 4

Printed by Martins of Berwick, bound by Hunter and Foulis in Great Britain.

Contents.

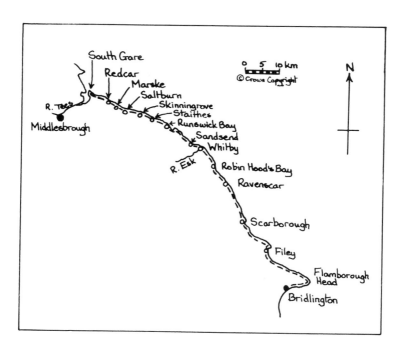

INTRODUCTION.

Yorkshire presents a cruel face to the sea. From the Tees to Bridlington there is a succession of towering cliffs and rocky scaurs, with tiny harbours or beaching points here and there. The villages and towns that have grown up around these havens are fairly easily reached by road (in most cases). Between them the roads sensibly veer inland, but this means that the grandeur of Yorkshire's cliffs is largely unseen. To appreciate it, you need to leave the roads behind and take to the coastal footpath. This guide is to help you do this, by providing enough information to enable you to find your way, together with notes on things you may see as you go.

The cliffs of Ravenscar.

The villages and towns are not ignored. They are worthy of exploration, being each full of individual character and charm. Take your time here, rather than dashing through on your way to somewhere else. The guide will perhaps answer some of the questions that may arise as you look around.

Whitby

Much of the route coincides with the coastal section of the Cleveland Way, between Saltburn and Filey. This makes route-finding much easier, for this popular long-distance path is well-trodden and sign-posted. But this is not so much a guide for the collector of miles, as one for those who want to take time to explore: an afternoon looking at the mining remains of Kettleness, say, or wandering around the ghauts of Whitby, rather than hurrying from Runswick Bay to Robin Hood's Bay in just one day. For this reason the guides offer no set timetable or itinerary. Do what suits you — and the weather!

Most map-sections start or end at a convenient point so that you can use alternative routes or public transport to return to your starting place. Sometimes you may wish to link several sections together for a longer walk. At others you may want to linger in a particular place.

There are delightful villages — Staithes, Runswick Bay, Robin Hood's Bay — that cling precariously to the foot of the cliffs where headlands provide shelter from the northerly winds of winter. The lack of space on the slopes has given rise to a picturesque cramming together, a welter of narrow alleys and red-pantiled roofs, an abundance of colourful but tiny gardens and window-boxes to make the most of the sun.

The towns are also positioned where there is shelter from the north: Whitby huddles in the narrow mouth of the river Esk; Scarborough, Filey and Bridlington shelter on the south side of headlands. Redcar appears to break the rule, but here offshore scars protect the town from the full force of the sea, if not from the wind. The genuine exception is Saltburn. But this is the creation of the Railway Age, when Victorian planners ignored the age-old wisdom and built on the clifftops rather than in the sheltered ravine of Old Saltburn.

The towns display very different characteristics: Scarborough Bridlington and Redcar are unashamedly commercial, serving the recreation needs of industrial areas inland, and very different as the seasons pass. Whitby, although cut off by the moors, has capitalised on its charm and history, and is active and welcoming throughout the year, whatever the weather. Filey presents a family resort atmosphere — refinement without snootiness. Saltburn is discovering that its Victorian style fits well into modern tastes for nostalgia. All of them have changed their ways to suit the leisure market.

Robin Hood's Bay.

But the traditions survive too. Each haven, whether a tiny inlet on the coast or a formal harbour has its fleet of fishing boats, remnant of centuries of fishing. Bridlington, Scarborough and Whitby have trawlers for deep-sea fishing and welcome boats from many parts of the country as they follow the fish. The smaller places all have a number of cobles, the traditional north-east fishing boat, suitable for launching from beaches, together with the tractors and trailers that go with them. Many places still have the life-boats that this inhospitable coast still makes so necessary.

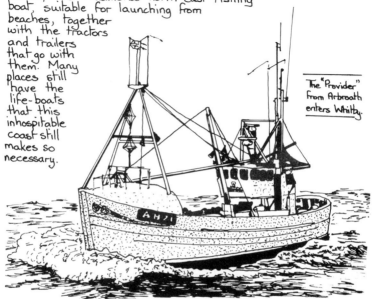

The "Provider" from Arbroath enters Whitby.

Other industry has left its mark on the coast north of Whitby. Here the rocks of the cliffs are mineral-rich. There are alum shales, stone, iron, a little coal, jet and cementstone. So the cliffs were systematically destroyed for their minerals, at Sandsend, Kettleness and Boulby. The scars, and the few remains, make fascinating exploring for the careful walker. Let your imagination play on what it must have been like to work on these exposed clifftop sites – or on the sailing ships that moored at the foot of the cliffs to receive the ores. Most industrial building has gone. At Skinningrove the steel works remains, rolling special sections, and at Boulby a deep mine extracts potash from under the North Sea. But the chemical and steel industries have not moved far, and their presence is seen (and smelled) near the mouth of the Tees.

This coast has always been vulnerable to invasion across the North Sea. The Danes and Vikings came this way, and left their mark in Yorkshire place-names, dialect and building styles as well as in the genes. Flamborough is still referred to as Little Denmark, and Yorkshire shepherds still count their sheep in Danish.

The Romans set a chain of warning signal stations along the coast, at Saltburn, Goldsborough, Ravenscar, Scarborough and Filey (and probably on other headlands now claimed by the sea or by industrial foraging).

Scarborough, with its readily defendable headland, developed its castle — but still received the attentions of Tostig and Harald Hadrada in 1066, of Paul Jones the American in 1779 and of the German Imperial Navy in 1914.

The Second World War saw a renewed threat from across the German Ocean, and pillboxes and military camps dotted this coastline. Their remains still litter the shore in places, but the inexorable process of coastal erosion is gradually taking them away.

Whitby's Abbey represents the cultural side of history, playing a significant rôle in the early Christian mission to this country. Destroyed by the Danes, it was refounded by Normans, and lasted until the Dissolution in 1549, a centre for economic as well as religious development.

Kettleness

Much later, the railways brought a new wave of industrial opportunities, and encouraged the growth of today's major industry: tourism and holidays. Two of the coastal lines have closed, but the path meets them from time to time, either using them directly, as at Sandsend, or suggesting their use as an alternative or return route.

THE GUIDE

includes a continuous strip map of the coast, to about 1:45 000 scale, from South Gare (Cleveland) to Bridlington (Humberside). These were both in Yorkshire before the counties were reorganised, so I make no apology for the title!

There are notes to help you follow the path (indicated by *) with suggested alternatives or digressions (✳). Comments about things to be seen along the way are prefaced with ●.

It is not intended as a single long-distance walk: much more of the coastal character can be appreciated by a series of short walks, taking time to stop, look and explore. The buses and trains that serve the coast allow a wide range of one-way walks if carefully planned.

RIGHTS OF WAY, CLIFFS, TIDES AND COASTAL WALKING

The route indicated on the sketch map is NOT evidence of a right of way. Between Saltburn and Filey the Cleveland Way does provide a continuous right of way. South of Filey the coastal path is fragmentary, with some parts dedicated and some not. In some places there are permissive paths, which walkers may use without asking the owner each time (such as the Whitby to Scarborough Railway).

Cliff-path between Stoupe Beck and Boggle Hole

Cliff walking requires care, of course. You should stop to admire the scenery! The paths are frequently near the edge of the cliffs, sometimes on the inside of a hedge or fence, sometimes on the outside. Some people do not enjoy such situations. Erosion is another menace. Not the erosion caused by many feet, but the persistent action of weather and the sea nibbling at the cliffs, taking the paths away. Here and there diversions are necessary.

Walking along the edge of the cliffs in the dark is NOT recommended!

Cliff-walking is also very tiring, unexpectedly so for some people. The paths do go up and down a great deal, even if they do not reach a great height. In places the slopes are so steep that there are steps or even ladders.

If you digress from the main path you will find these problems amplified. There are places where the OS maps show a path (even rights of way), where the evidence on the spot is very hard to find, or where such paths as do exist are steep or very overgrown, making them unsuitable for the average walker.

Runswick Bay.

In places the recommended route is along the shore. This, between the tide-lines, is the property of the Crown, and there is seldom any objection to its use as a thoroughfare on foot. But it is not always passable or safe. Choose the time of your trips carefully. Avoid being trapped against cliffs by the incoming tide.

Notes on route-finding are brief. The sea and cliffs are fairly reliable guides to the coastline. There is little scope for mistakes, provided that you know whether you should be below the cliffs or on top of them!

Rights of way ARE indicated on Ordnance Survey maps. Useful
sheets are:
   1:50 000   Sheet 93, Middlesbrough and Darlington
              Sheet 94, Whitby
              Sheet 101, Scarborough and Bridlington.
   1:25 000   Outdoor Leisure Map: North York Moors East.

Please respect the life of the countryside and shore:
Shut gates.
Keep dogs under control. Where there is livestock keep them
on a lead.
Stay on the path. Do not wander on the crops. Grass is
a very expensive and important crop.
Guard against fire.
Leave farm machinery, crops and livestock alone.
Do not interfere with boats, launching tractors or other
fishing apparatus.
Take your litter home with you. Even a ring-pull or a
plastic bag can kill.
Respect wildlife: animals, plants and trees. There is
much to see, especially birds. Look, but do not interfere.

Cobles on the beach, Marske.

SENSIBLE WEAR:

The weather along the coast can change rapidly. Rain
(or snow) can reach you from the horizon more quickly
than you can walk ½ a mile to shelter. Even a hot day
in summer can become chilly and foggy as cool sea
air creeps in under still warm air from the land. This
coast is notorious for its roaks.
So be prepared. Carry a cagoule and a pullover as
well as your swim-wear and suntan cream in summer.
In winter the wind can come straight from the Arctic.
Thermal wear, anoraks, woollen hats and mittens can
be essential, even when the sun shines.

12.

Sensible footwear needs thought too. Heavy boots are not the best wear for soft sandy beaches. Rocks and clifftops require more than sandals or town shoes. Select your footwear to match the route chosen.

Also remember a watch: tides and buses wait for no-one. Binoculars are also very useful, not only for watching birds but also to observe the passing shipping.

ACCOMMODATION

There are villages every few miles along the coast, with inns and bed-and-breakfast accommodation. In summer this can be heavily booked, so it is wise to plan ahead. There are also centres where cottages, caravans or chalets can be hired. The information centres may be able to help with addresses and telephone numbers.

There are youth hostels at Saltburn, Boggle Hole, Whitby and Scalby Mills.

North of Whitby campsites are scarce. There is one at Lythe. Caravanners fare somewhat better, at Saltburn, Staithes and Hinderwell.

South of Whitby the situation is different. This is summer holiday country, with plentiful sites for camping and caravanning.

South Bay Cliff Lift, Scarborough.

13.

Bus Links

A number of local routes connect Middlesbrough, Redcar and Saltburn. Saltburn has a service to Loftus, as has Skinningrove. These link to the major route to Whitby from Middlesbrough (via Guisborough). This visits Staithes, Runswick Bay and Sandsend, with extra buses in summer.

Whitby has local buses, and an express service across the moors to Middlesbrough. Buses run to Robin Hood's Bay, and, less often, to Scarborough.

Ravenscar has an infrequent service to Scarborough through Cloughton.

Scarborough has local buses, including the seasonally open-top service along the seafront. Scarborough, Filey and Bridlington are linked by useful services, with more in summer when the holiday villages are in operation.

Flamborough is served by buses from Bridlington.

Redcar
Marske
Saltburn
Skinningrove
A174
Staithes
Middlesbrough
A173 Loftus
Runswick Bay
A174
Sandsend
Whitby
to A171
M'bro
Robin Hood's Bay
A171
Ravenscar
Cloughton
A170
Scarborough
A64
B1261
Filey
A1039
A165
Flamborough
Bridlington
to Hull
© Crown Copyright

All bus services are subject to changes of route, timing and operator. For up-to-date information contact bus companies in Middlesbrough, Whitby, Scarborough and Bridlington.

Local trains operate to Redcar, Marske & Saltburn, from Middlesbrough and Darlington

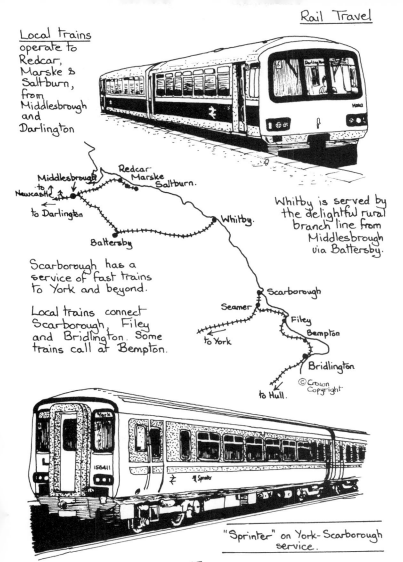

Whitby is served by the delightful rural branch line from Middlesbrough via Battersby.

Scarborough has a service of fast trains to York and beyond.

Local trains connect Scarborough, Filey and Bridlington. Some trains call at Bempton.

© Crown Copyright

"Sprinter" on York-Scarborough service.

15.

The South Gare

• Beside the lighthouse is the <u>Fog Horn</u>.

• The lighthouse, unusually, is not operated by Trinity House, but by the Tees and Hartlepool Port Authority. It was built of cast iron and concrete in 1884. It flashes for three seconds in every ten when lit.

• The whole <u>South Gare</u>, 4km (2½ miles) of it from Warrenby, is artificial. After a great storm in 1861 when upwards of fifty vessels were wrecked on the sand-bar between Redcar and Hartlepool, two breakwaters were built on the banks of the Tees. A railway line was built to bring slag from the iron and steel works of Teesside, and the Gare was built out into the estuary. Traces of the railway can still be seen near the coastguard station. It was completed in 1888, but continual work is needed to prevent the sea reclaiming it.

The road from Warrenby, and the Gare itself, are private. The public is only admitted by courtesy of British Steel and the Port Authority.

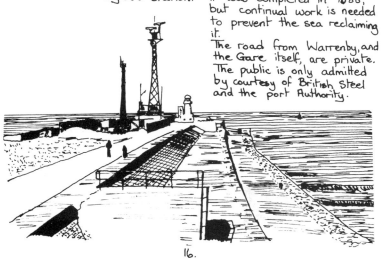

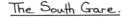

- The River Tees, with Hartlepool, is one of the busiest ports in the U.K. Enormous tonnages of oil come and go from the great refineries visible upriver; iron ore comes to the Redcar Ore Terminal; and much general cargo in the coasters and container vessels that frequently ply in and out. There are always large ships at anchor in Tees Bay. Their movements are controlled by the port authority. The <u>coastguard station</u> on the Gare monitors all the activity. Pilot cutters dash in and out from their mooring near the lifeboat station. A powerful boat completely fills the RNLI shed, a reminder that the sea is often far from benign. One of the crew is usually on hand if you wish to visit the <u>lifeboat house</u>.

South Gare to Redcar

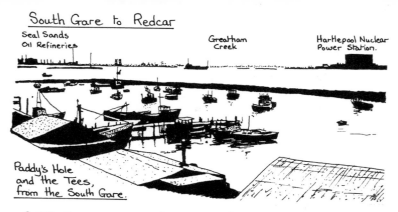

Seal Sands
Oil Refineries

Greatham
Creek

Hartlepool Nuclear
Power Station.

Paddy's Hole
and the Tees,
from the South Gare.

- The Gare is a marvellous viewpoint. On a clear day you can see well up the coast. Opposite you is the small promontory of the North Gare. Beyond it stretch the sands of Seaton Carew, with the town and busy port of Hartlepool beyond. Closer at hand, the large rectangular box to the west is the nuclear power station. Greatham Creek separates it from Seal Sands, reclaimed from the estuary, which the oil companies have covered with refineries. To the south is British Steel Redcar, with huge unloading gantries alongside the river. Beyond, on the horizon, are the Cleveland Hills. Eastwards the beach stretches out to Redcar and on towards an abrupt terminus at Saltburn's Hunt Cliff.

British Steel

South Gare to Redcar

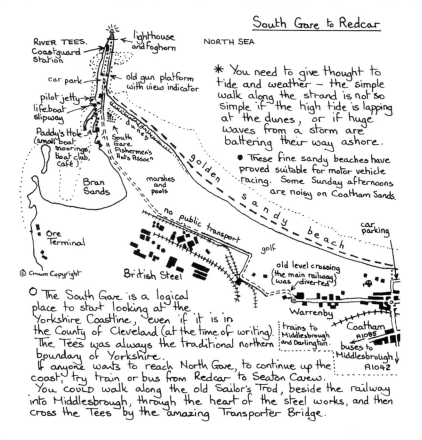

NORTH SEA

RIVER TEES. Coastguard Station

lighthouse and foghorn

car park

old gun platform with view indicator

pilot jetty

lifeboat slipway

Paddy's Hole (small boat moorings, boat club, café)

South Gare Fishermen's Huts Assoc'n

dunes

Bran Sands

marshes and pools

golden sandy beach

Ore Terminal

© Crown Copyright

British Steel

no public transport

golf

old level crossing (the main railway was diverted)

car parking

Warrenby

trains to Middlesbrough and Darlington

Coatham A1085

buses to Middlesbrough A1042

* You need to give thought to tide and weather — the simple walk along the strand is not so simple if the high tide is lapping at the dunes, or if huge waves from a storm are battering their way ashore.

• These fine sandy beaches have proved suitable for motor vehicle racing. Some Sunday afternoons are noisy on Coatham Sands.

O The South Gare is a logical place to start looking at the Yorkshire Coastline, even if it is in the County of Cleveland (at the time of writing). The Tees was always the traditional northern boundary of Yorkshire.
If anyone wants to reach North Gare, to continue up the coast, try train or bus from Redcar to Seaton Carew.
You could walk along the old Sailor's Trod, beside the railway into Middlesbrough, through the heart of the steel works, and then cross the Tees by the amazing Transporter Bridge.

19.

Redcar to Marske

• Redcar has a full range of shops, plus accommodation, entertainment and transport. Trains run to Middlesbrough and Darlington, and to Saltburn. Buses run to all kinds of local destinations, and also Middlesbrough and Saltburn.

The town is protected from the worst efforts of the North Sea by the two bands of rocks stretching well out to sea. They stand starkly proud at low tide (offering an unusual view-point), and convert the rollers into crashing surf when the water is high. So although Redcar has no formal harbour it does provide shelter for a fleet of cobles and other small boats. These are often parked at the head of the beach, or along the Esplanade.

The flashing red light on the front of Marks and Spencer is a beacon for the safe way in between the two sets of rocks.

Low tide on the East Flashes

• Redcar boasts two lifeboat stations. The older is now the Zetland Museum, which houses the oldest surviving lifeboat, the "Zetland". This was built in North Shields in 1800, and served for 78 years from 1802 until 1880, being instrumental in the saving of many lives on this rough coast, where many vessels have foundered (and still do). The current lifeboat station, just to the west, is a modern building very different in design from the more traditional buildings dotted along this coast.

20.

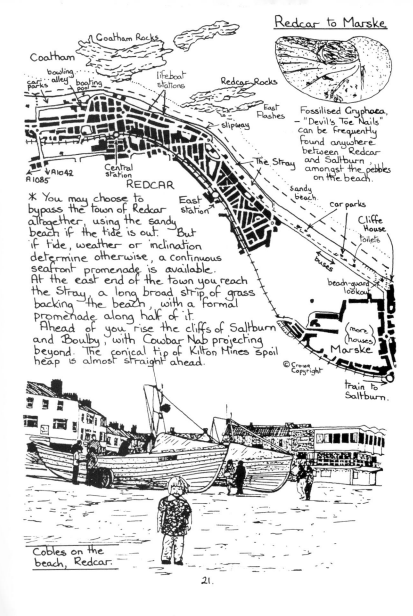

Redcar to Marske

Coatham Rocks

Coatham

bowling alley
car parks
boating pool
lifeboat stations

Redcar Rocks

East Flashes

slipway

A1042
A1085
Central station
REDCAR

East station

The Stray

sandy beach

car parks

Cliffe House
toilets

buses

beach-guard lookout

(more) houses
Marske

© Crown Copyright

train to Saltburn.

Fossilised Gryphaea, – "Devil's Toe Nails" can be frequently found anywhere between Redcar and Saltburn, amongst the pebbles on the beach.

* You may choose to bypass the town of Redcar altogether, using the sandy beach if the tide is out. But if tide, weather or inclination determine otherwise, a continuous seafront promenade is available.
At the east end of the town you reach the Stray, a long broad strip of grass backing the beach, with a formal promenade along half of it.
Ahead of you rise the cliffs of Saltburn and Boulby, with Cowbar Nab projecting beyond. The conical tip of Kilton Mines spoil heap is almost straight ahead.

Cobles on the beach, Redcar.

21.

Marske to Saltburn

• The haven of <u>Marske</u> is hidden from the casual passerby or motorist. The old High Street is not the present thoroughfare, but runs quietly down into a sheltered hollow, Spout Beck Chine. The haven still boasts a fleet of cobles. These normally rest on the open beach, being pulled up into shelter when the sea threatens.

• <u>Cliffe House</u> (above) was built by the Pease family, Cleveland Ironmasters, in the middle of the nineteenth century. It was used by the Holiday Fellowship from the 1930's until 1974. After a sad interlude of neglect, fire, and vandalism, it was acquired by the Church Army. Now it forms the centre of a home for elderly people.

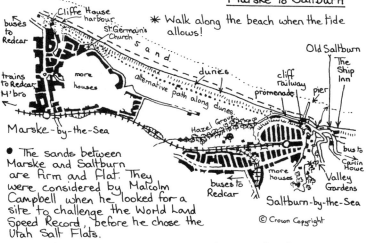

* Walk along the beach when the tide allows!

© Crown Copyright

- The sands between Marske and Saltburn are firm and flat. They were considered by Malcolm Campbell when he looked for a site to challenge the World Land Speed Record, before he chose the Utah Salt Flats.

- St. Germain's Church now consists just of a tower in a churchyard. But this is an ancient church site, dating from Saxon times. The tower is mainly Norman, from about 1160. The church fell into disrepair, and was blown up and rebuilt in 1821. But the austere new building was rendered redundant by the larger Parish Church. Derelict again, it was demolished in the 1950's.

Old Saltburn and Hunt Cliff.

23.

Saltburn-by-the-Sea

- Saltburn is Victorian. It was the creation of Henry Pease, a great entrepreneur of the time. He saw its potential as a resort for the new industrial areas of Teesside. The Stockton and Darlington Railway was extended into the centre of the new town on the clifftop, and terminated at a private platform in the railway hotel – the Zetland. The Saltburn Improvement Company induced others to build the characteristic row of tall houses along Marine Parade. But a down-turn in the iron industry blighted the hopes of the Company, and Saltburn never did acquire the status it sought. But now, a century on, the town is starting to take a new pride in its origins. There are Victorian weeks in summer, when shops and townsfolk dress up in period costume, and Victoria & Albert are seen taking the air on the pier. The station area has been redeveloped with new shops and the town is seizing its identity again.

There are, too, still trains to Redcar, Middlesbrough and Darlington. (–and buses too).

Things to note or visit:
- the Valley Gardens, below the town alongside Skelton Beck,
- the miniature railway in the gardens,
- the shopfronts of the town, with their ornate ironworks and awnings,
- the prospect of Huntcliff ahead! – and
- the beach of fine sand, where you can cool your hot feet in the surf :–

Saltburn

● Saltburn Pier is the last remaining pleasure pier on the "Yorkshire" coast. It was originally much longer (450 metres when built in 1869). It has had gaps torn in it – by the sailing ship "Ovenbeg" in 1924 and by the military during World War II. The restored pier was damaged by the fierce seas of 1952, but survived until 1974. Then, just after the Council had agreed to renovate it, a storm carried away the pier head. Local people fought against total demolition, and it was rebuilt in its present form.

● The cliff railway was built in 1884, replacing a rickety vertical hoist.

The two cars counterbalance each other. They are linked by a cable over a brake drum at the top, and each has a large water tank. Water is added to the car at the top until it is heavy enough to raise the other car! Simple! The water is then pumped back up the slope to be used again. Attendants at top and bottom fasten the doors on the outside. It is cheap, effective and safe. Try it!

Saltburn Cliff Railway and Pier

Saltburn to Hunt Cliff

Old Saltburn : "The Ship".

• The Ship probably dates from around 1550, and served the community of fishermen, alum-workers, smugglers and wreckers that inhabited Old Saltburn. The place was notorious for smuggling, and the row of cottages on Hunt Cliff were built for the coastguard to try to curtail the trade. The shore was the scene of many wrecks as sailing vessels found themselves embayed by adverse winds. In 1881 so many bodies were being washed ashore that a mortuary was built opposite the Ship Inn (where the coroner's court would sit).

• Hunt Cliff is an excellent vantage point. The Romans had a signal station there, one of a coastal chain. (The next south is at Goldsborough). The site was excavated in 1911, but has since been claimed by the North Sea. But do not forget to admire the view. You can see far up the Durham coastline, well beyond Hartlepool. There is the dramatic skyline of industrial Teesside, and to the south the bowl scooped out by Skelton Beck, ringed by the railway that once served the numerous ironstone mines.

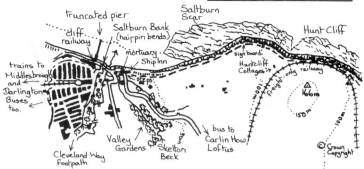

* From the beach, walk past the small hillock of Cat Nab, and the mortuary to the Ship Inn. A path goes steeply up behind the inn, then follows a well-defined line by the field boundaries behind the cliff edge. These rise to more than 100 metres (300'), so don't lean over too far while looking at birds nesting on the ledges below! (Birds here include cormorants). But do remember to look back at the view from time to time (– a good excuse for a rest!). Go on past the notice that tells you about the Roman signal station, to reach the railway.

Hunt Cliff (from the railway).

27.

Hunt Cliff to Skinningrove

A train of potash from Boulby snakes its way along the edge of Huntcliff, 100 metres above the sea.

● This spectacular <u>railway</u> was opened in 1867, looping round over Huntcliff in order to serve ironstone mines there. <u>Skinningrove Ironworks</u> added to its traffic from 1873, and kept it going after passenger services ceased in 1960. Now the traffic from the potash mine (opened in the 1970's) makes it a busy line. (The line had to be relaid beyond Carlin How, across Kilton viaduct and past Loftus to Boulby).

There used to be a zig-zag branch line down from Carlin Howe to Skinningrove. It must have been an amazing sight to watch steam engines pulling loaded iron-ore trains up the 1 in 28 gradient, with ore from the valley mines.

The iron works also had an incline railway down onto the jetty. You may be able to find traces at the incline foot.

● <u>Skinningrove</u> almost died as a village after the mines closed. It was scheduled for run-down of services and non-renewal of housing. But the residents had other ideas and now it has some new houses and a future. A cluster of boats use the harbour, and pigeon lofts dot the hillside below the looming presence of the steel works.

The beck is a lurid orange colour. This is <u>not</u> sewage, but the result of drainage from ironstone workings in the valley. You may see where it enters the beck if you keep watch as you walk up the lane towards the main road.

28.

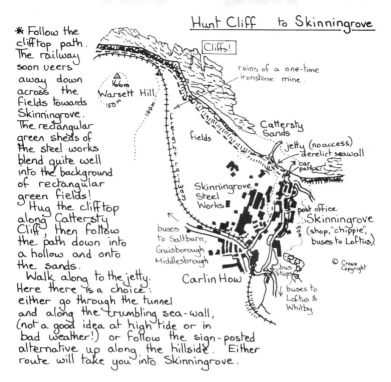

* Follow the clifftop path. The railway soon veers away down across the fields towards Skinningrove. The rectangular green sheds of the steel works blend quite well into the background of rectangular green fields!

Hug the clifftop along Cattersty Cliff, then follow the path down into a hollow and onto the sands.

Walk along to the jetty. Here there is a choice: either go through the tunnel and along the crumbling sea-wall, (not a good idea at high tide or in bad weather!) or follow the sign-posted alternative up along the hillside. Either route will take you into Skinningrove.

Cliffs!

ruins of a one-time ironstone mine.

△ 66m
Warsett Hill
150m

Cattersty Sands

fields

jetty (no access)
derelict seawall
car park

Skinningrove Steel Works

post office

Skinningrove
(shop, "chippie", buses to Loftus).

© Crown Copyright

buses to Saltburn, Guisborough, Middlesbrough

Carlin How

bus stops

buses to Loftus & Whitby

Down to Cattersty Sands.

29.

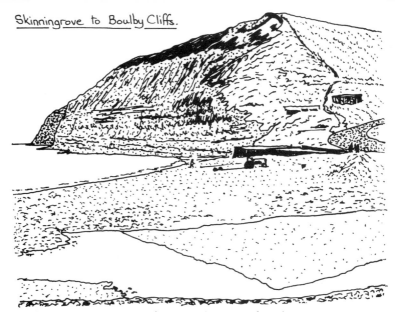

* Cross Kilton Beck by the road-bridge. A path goes directly up
<u>Hummersea Cliff</u> (above). Follow it up, remembering to look
back at the views of Skinningrove and the <u>harbour</u> (below),
and walk along the clifftop until directed inland near Hummersea Farm. Join a cart-track up towards the heights of Boulby
Cliff. This becomes a path again to wend a way along the lip
of the quarries. Take care!

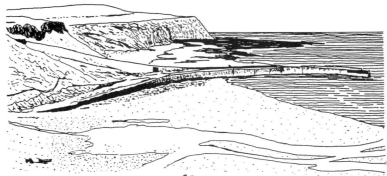

car park
boats huts
Hummersea Scar
Hummersea Port & Alum House
Cliffs!
disused quarries

Steel Works

Hummersea Farm

Snilah Pond

very steep hill

© Crown Copyright

Fields

quiet lane

(appalling surface!)

Rockcliff Farm

A 213

police radio transmitter

bus stops at foot of bank

→ buses to Boulby, Staithes and Whitby.

Cowbar Nab →

Staithes

Hinderwell Beacon ↓

✲ Below Hummersea Farm, where you turn inland, a steep path goes down to Hummersea Port. Here a gap in the rocks allowed boats to tie up at the Alum House, to exchange cargoes. It must have been a risky business! More details are given in the Cleveland Industrial Heritage Trail leaflets.

Boulby Cliff quarries.

31.

Boulby : Mining.

- Boulby and mining go together. As you walk over the clifftop you cannot fail to notice the huge quarries. A 200 metre wide strip, 100 metres high, has been gouged away in man's search for minerals. Iron, alum and jet are found in bands at the lower levels, coal and limestone higher up. I have seen it look like Dante's Inferno on a hot summer's day, when the bituminous seams have caught fire, wreathing the cliff in smoke and red fire.

  Try to imagine what it must have been like when it was being worked. There would have been great heaps of alum, burning in its own oil for almost a year before being leached in great tanks. The stench of boiled seaweed and urine, used to add potassium or ammonium to the brew, would have mingled with the steam and smoke. Imagine too what it must have been like to work here, on the exposed cliff-face, especially in winter.

  If you explore the quarries, do take great care — be wary of the cliff-faces, and of pits and levels.

700'
(210m)
down
to the sea

32.

• Although the cliff quarries are now peaceful, men are still at work extracting minerals. More than a kilometre below your feet is the new <u>potash mine</u>, opened in 1974. The mine stretches far out under the sea, producing mainly potash for the fertiliser and chemical industries, and also some salt as a by-product (The mine roadways are driven through the salt under the potash layer, as the salt is more stable at the immense pressures at that depth). Nearly all the chemicals leave along the re-opened railway towards Teesside. The surface buildings have made few friends, being visible for considerable distances, despite screens of trees and careful painting.

<u>Boulby</u>

33.

Boulby Cliffs to Staithes

* The path goes on along the rim of the quarries, and then clearly turns downhill, quite steeply, once they are passed. You descend almost to the sea-cliffs, then a footpath takes you into the hamlet of Boulby: only a few houses but in a spectacular location. Continue down the lane, past the few houses and a junction, to the corner at the bottom....

Roxby Beck

Boulby Cliff to Staithes

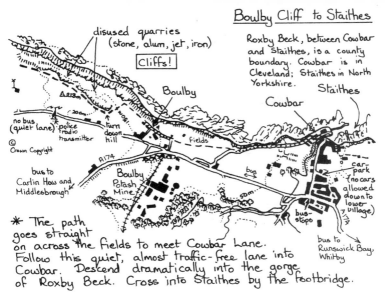

disused quarries (stone, alum, jet, iron)

Cliffs!

Boulby

Roxby Beck, between Cowbar and Staithes, is a county boundary. Cowbar is in Cleveland; Staithes in North Yorkshire.

Staithes

Cowbar

no bus (quiet lane)
police
radio
transmitter

© Crown Copyright

turn down hill

fields

bus to Carlin How and Middlesbrough

Boulby Potash Mine

A174

bus ←

car-park (no cars allowed down to lower village)

bus-stops

bus to Runswick Bay, Whitby

* The path goes straight on across the fields to meet Cowbar Lane. Follow this quiet, almost traffic-free lane into Cowbar. Descend dramatically into the gorge of Roxby Beck. Cross into Staithes by the footbridge.

Retrospect from Cowbar Lane

35.

Staithes

• The original fishing village is crammed onto a shelf between the sea and the cliff, only just above sea-level. A newer village has grown up the hill, near the erstwhile railway station (now the main car-park) and the main road. Vehicular access to the lower village is restricted, and there is no parking down there. The reason is obvious — almost every available space has been used for building, leaving only a narrow lane for access, and a picturesque cluster of pantiled cottages. It is still, in part, a fishing village. The double-enders are still moored above the bridge, with the square-sterned cobles below. But it is also a tourist village in summer, very understandably, and has shops and artist's studios and places to eat and stay. It is a place full of charm, especially in early morning or early evening when it is quiet. In bad weather from the north-east it can take a fearful pounding from the sea, despite the two long breakwaters and the massive sea-wall. The "Cod and Lobster" on the sea-wall has been damaged several times (In 1953 a storm broke in and stole all the bottled stock, yielding some of it back to beach-combers over the following days. On another occasion it was a ship's bowsprit that broke in — through a window!).

        • Across the beck is <u>Cowbar</u> — several clusters of houses and the lifeboat station huddling under the protection of Cowbar Nab.

Cobles moored at the mouth of Staithes Beck.

● At low tide the broad wave-cut platform of Penny Steel is revealed below the cliffs east of the village. It can be explored for some way round the headland and towards Old Nab. But do beware of the tide! It rushes in quickly over the flat platform, and there is no escape up the cliffs between Staithes and Port Mulgrave (2 km away).

37.

Staithes to Runswick Bay

* Church Street, near the 'Cod + Lobster' is the way out of the village to the south. The road climbs steeply, and becomes a track. This turns left onto the level fields and heads east, one or two fields back from the cliffs. You reach the cliff edge again beyond Old Nab, where you climb quite sharply up Quarry Bank. There are fine views back from here. The cliff-top path runs round the rim of Brackenberry Wyke, skirting past the dome of Hinderwell Beacon (an Elizabethan Early Warning Station). You pass above the tiny harbour of Port Mulgrave, tucked into the corner of Rosedale Wyke. A road here offers an escape inland to Hinderwell, for the weary). There are also paths down to the harbour for those who have the energy and the inclination to explore.

For those continuing to Runswick, a path follows the fields' edge round Rosedale Wyke onto Lingrow Cliffs, (100m above the sea). Shortly before you reach the corner of Runswick Bay, a sharp right turn is made at a small pond. A field path takes you straightforwardly to Runswick Bank Top.

Kettleness

Rosedale Wyke and Lingrow.

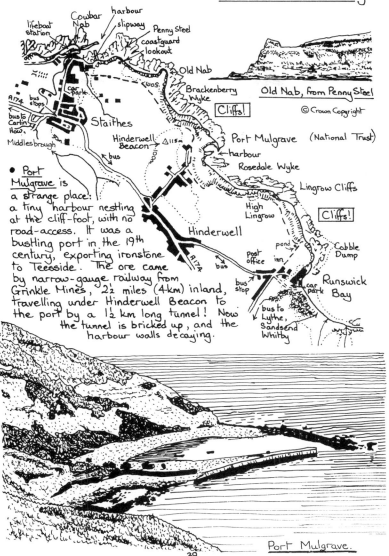

lifeboat station
Cowbar Nab
harbour
slipway
Penny Steel
coastguard lookout

Old Nab

Old Nab, from Penny Steel
© Crown Copyright

car park
A174
bus stops
bus to Carlin How, Middlesbrough

WOS.

Brackenberry Wyke

Cliffs!

Staithes

Hinderwell Beacon △115

Port Mulgrave (National Trust)
← harbour
Rosedale Wyke

100'

bus

Lingrow Cliffs

High Lingrow

Cliffs!

• Port Mulgrave is
a strange place:
a tiny harbour nestling
at the cliff-foot, with no
road-access. It was a
bustling port in the 19th
century, exporting ironstone
to Teesside. The ore came
by narrow-gauge railway from
Grinkle Mines, 2½ miles (4km) inland,
travelling under Hinderwell Beacon to
the port by a 1½ km long tunnel! Now
the tunnel is bricked up, and the
harbour walls decaying.

Hinderwell

A174
bus
post office
pond
inn

Cobble Dump

bus stop
bus to Lythe, Sandsend, Whitby

car park
Runswick Bay

Port Mulgrave.

• The older part of the village at Runswick Bay is tucked away at the foot of the cliff, invisible to those arriving by road, or on foot from the north. Only as you descend the bank - by the 1 in 4 road or the footway from the top carpark (the old road) - does the village come into view. The cliff protects it from the northerly winds, and its sunny south-facing aspect makes it an ideal seaside residence (it even boasts a palm tree - by the Thatched Cottage). So it was an early victim of the move by the affluent to obtain second homes by the sea. By the 1940's the fishing had almost all gone and the village had given itself over to the holiday business. Now it only has about 40 all-year residents. But it is seldom deserted. Even in winter it has many visitors, and in summer parking is a problem for the tardy. Then the beach - of good sand - is thronged with sun-bathers and families, and the sea with sailing boats, wind-surfers and swimmers.

Fishing boats parked atop the seawall.

• The picturesque village, with its delightful gardens, is a place of mixtures: old and new; picture windows and Victorian sashes; tile and slate; flat roofs and thatch; cheap and expensive; brash and refined. But everywhere has one common feature: the magnificent view round the Bay to Kettleness.

The village is not the original. That slid into the sea one night in 1664, leaving only one house intact but—fortunately—with little loss of life. The village was rebuilt, further away from the point, on the present site. But the dangers of land-slip remain. The seawalls help, but even the massive wall at the foot of the carpark is being undermined. Little resists the sea permanently.

• The lifeboat station (opposite) no longer houses a RNLI boat. The village operates its own inshore rescue boat.

There is an excellent detailed guide to the village in the 'Heritage Coast' leaflet series. (from information offices or National Park centres).

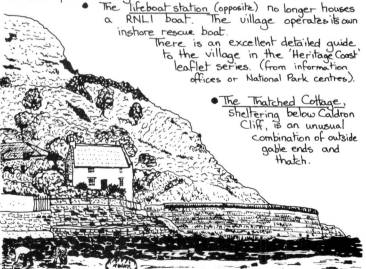

• The Thatched Cottage, sheltering below Caldron Cliff, is an unusual combination of outside gable ends and thatch.

Runswick Bay

● The shore is a delight.
Going south, there is first the
<u>sand</u>, smooth and fine, great
for sand-castles and sunbathing.

Then come the <u>pebbles</u>. Unlike
those on many beaches, these
are immensely varied in colour
and type. There are reds & greens,
blues and browns, black & white.
Some are multicoloured, some are
plain. Some are veined in startling
contrast. Ponder their origins.

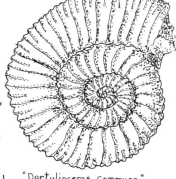

"Dactylioceras commune"

Beyond the sailing club-house
the beach is backed by a cliff
(low at first) of jet shales capped
with heavy clay. In the cliff front are several caverns – some
naturally caused by erosion, some opened out in pursuit of
jet. These are the <u>Hob Holes</u>, reputedly home to a hob who
could cure whooping cough.

Beyond Claymoor Beck the sand gives way to a flat, wave-
cut platform of rock. Gently tilted, this shows a gradual
succession of Upper Lias rocks. You walk first on the Grey
Shales, that contain many <u>fossils</u> for the observant to spot.
The most obvious are the whorls of <u>ammonites</u> (as above)
and the long, round-tapered cones of <u>belemnites</u>.

View over the hedge at the bank-top.

Claymoor Beck and Hob Holes

● The ammonites (and their impressions) can be found on the surface of the grey stone. Some up to 15cm diameter are easily found. Please do not try to chip them from their beds —they will probably disintegrate if you try. You may be fortunate enough to find some loose amongst debris from the cliffs at the top of the beach.

The red lumps scattered in a wide band across the rock are called sideritic concretions.

Fossil hunting can claim your attention for some time — ALWAYS keep an eye on the tide!

Runswick Bay to Kettleness

<u>Runswick Bay seen from the path up Claymoor End</u>

* If you get the tide wrong and there is a high sea running onto the beach, you will have to do something other than walk to Hob Holes. There is no short alternative route. Perhaps this is the time to explore Runswick village (unless you are stuck up Claymoor Beck of course!)

<u>Catbeck Hill</u> with <u>Kettleness beyond</u>. Note how the rock changes as you reach the point (This why there <u>is</u> a point!).

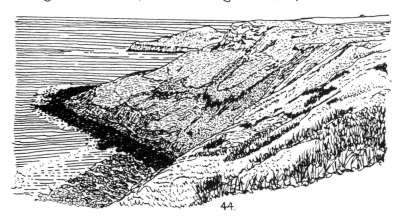

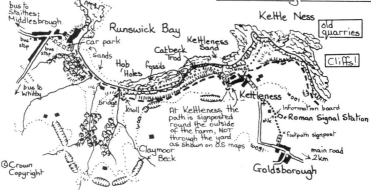

@Crown
Copyright

* From Runswick Banktop descend to the sea-wall. Use either the
stepped footpath beside the 1 in 4 road, or the longer zigzag route
of the old road (now a footpath).

If you have judged the tide right you will be able to descend
onto the beach and trudge along the sand southwards. The
wooden dwellings on your right, amongst the scrub, are holiday
homes, built before the era of planning regulations. The last,
the yacht club-house is cheerfully painted. Make your way
past the Hob Holes to the gap in the cliffs where Claymoor
Beck splashes down onto the beach.

If you want to take the high road, turn up the beckside path
(discovering why it is so named) to a footbridge. Steps lead up the
flank of Claymoor End. The path turns up behind a little knoll
(a superb view-point), to reach the clifftop. Follow it along
towards Kettleness, enjoying the views. On your right you
may notice the course of the erstwhile Middlesbrough to Whitby
Railway. A path beside it is an alternative way to Kettleness.
* If the tide is favourable and you LIKE brambles, gorse and bracken,
then an alternative route from Hob Holes is along the beach. After
exploring for fossils you can clamber up onto the lower slopes of
Catbeck Hill. Catbeck Trod is an intermittent path, diagonally
up the slopes towards
Kettleness. The finish
is indistinct. Climb up
before the gulley of
Catbeck, which is an
unpleasant trap. This
route is for roughnecks
and masochists.

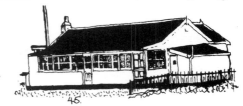

Kettleness

✻ A <u>Roman Signal Station</u> was sited on the hillside above Kettleness. If you want to visit it, go up the Goldsborough road almost to the church. A field path goes diagonally up to a stile, with the signal station just beyond. The excavated site has been covered with turf, so there is not much to see, except the view. From here you can see Boulby Rockcliff and Old Nab to the north,. Whitby and Ravenscar Peak to the south. The chain of signal stations was a 4th century attempt at an early warning system, signalling to the cavalry when invasion threatened. (The 'golf balls' on Fylingdales Moor do the nuclear equivalent). The Roman stations were overwhelmed by Saxon raiders after only about twenty years.

● Until 1829 there was much more of <u>Kettleness</u> <u>village</u>. One stormy December night the cliff washed away, carrying the village and the alum works with it. The villagers, unable to climb the moving cliff, escaped onto an alum boat moored offshore. The alum works was rebuilt, but there is little at the village now. Even the impressive railway station is a Scouts' centre, and the church is falling into ruin.

● The <u>steel post</u> with a ring, on Lucky Dog's Point (above), is for the coastguards to practise the use of breeches buoy and rockets.

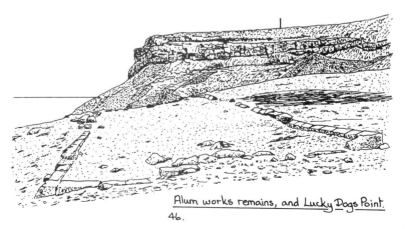

Alum works remains, and <u>Lucky Dogs Point.</u>

Kettle Ness from Lucky Dogs Point

✱ The Alum quarries on the Ness
can be visited. A path from the centre
of the hamlet goes north where the
Cleveland Way sign points east. A broad,
gently graded pannierway, it provides easy
access to the flat working area between the stump of headland
and the cliff behind. A slight embankment carries it across
towards the foundations of the alum house, on the brink of
the east cliffs. You may also spot stone channels that once
conducted the liquor from the leaching tanks to the alum
house. Little remains: anything removable has long since gone.
There is no easy way up the ring of cliffs except the way
that you came down.

47.

Kettleness to Sandsend.

Tellgreen Hill

✳ A Cleveland Way sign points the way over Lucky Dogs Point. You follow the cliff round until you meet the original route of the railway (see below) and the later cutting and tunnel. Go up the near bank of the cutting, and enjoy the clifftop march along to Tellgreen Hill. There the path naturally assumes a course one field-length up from the cliff (not as shown on OS maps). Superb views of Whitby and Sandsend open up. Across a stile, the path dives down steep steps through a wood, to meet the old railway line emerging from Sandsend Tunnel. Play trains past Sandsend Ness (see next pages) to Sandsend station. Steps take you down to the carpark on the site of the old alum house.

● The Middlesbrough to Whitby railway was started in 1866, but the work done by contractors was suspect. The company asked the North Eastern Railway to take over. What they found appalled them. The original works clung to the cliff-face between Kettleness and Sandsend, on a narrow shelf (just visible above — the thorn bushes mark it at this end), with only a short tunnel through the end of Tellgreen Hill. Some of this shelf was already collapsing during construction. The NER, more businesslike, built a short tunnel at Kettleness to bypass a collapsed shelf, and a much longer one (1½ km) under Ovalgate Cliff to Deepgrove. This still left a spectacular section on the cliff-face above Seavybog Hill. What a journey this must have been by train! You can still see some of the works — parts, including the line closed in 1958 are marked by thorn-scrub, and the tunnel mouths can still be seen (The tunnels have suffered subsidence and should NOT be entered).

48.

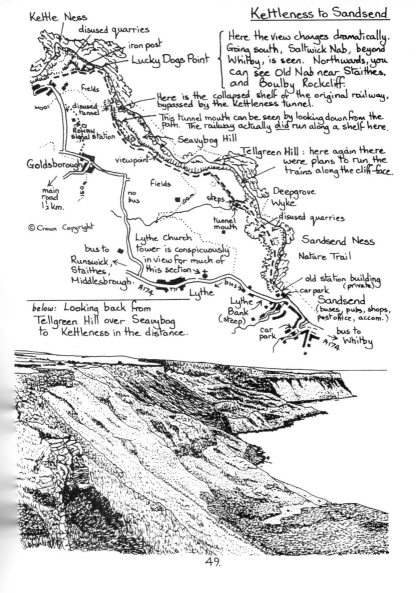

Kettleness to Sandsend

Kettle Ness

disused quarries

iron post

Lucky Dogs Point

fields

moor

disused tunnel

ROMAN signal station

Goldsborough

main road 1½ km.

© Crown Copyright

viewpoint

fields

no bus

Seavybog Hill

Here the view changes dramatically. Going south, Saltwick Nab, beyond Whitby, is seen. Northwards, you can see Old Nab near Staithes, and Boulby Rockcliff.

Here is the collapsed shelf of the original railway, bypassed by the Kettleness tunnel.

This tunnel mouth can be seen by looking down from the path. The railway actually _did_ run along a shelf here.

Tellgreen Hill : here again there were plans to run the trains along the cliff face.

Deepgrove Wyke

disused quarries

steps

tunnel mouth

Sandsend Ness

Nature Trail

bus to Runswick, Staithes, Middlesbrough.

Lythe church tower is conspicuously in view for much of this section

A174

Lythe

old station building (private)

car park

Sandsend (buses, pubs, shops, post office, accom.)

Lythe Bank (steep)

car park

bus to Whitby

A174

below: Looking back from Tellgreen Hill over Seavybog to Kettleness in the distance.

Sandsend Ness

● Here is another area extensively quarried in the 18th and 19th centuries. As well as alum, jet, cement and stone were extracted. The alum house was where the carpark is now. The alum industry collapsed in the 1860's, and the new railway took the opportunity to build a level track through the heart of the defunct workings. At that time this was a truly barren landscape with not a tree or bush — or even grass — to be seen. (You can see this in photographs by Frank Meadows Sutcliffe, the eminent Victorian photographer from Whitby.) Now the vegetation — and wildlife — is coming back.

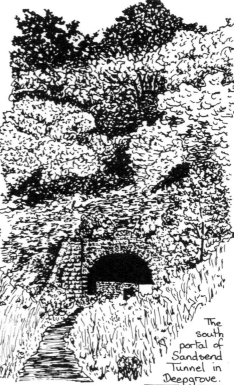

The south portal of Sandsend Tunnel in Deepgrove.

Sandsend Ness

The "railway" from Deepgrove

✳ As an alternative
to the railway you can follow the Nature Trail. Details can
be found in the National Park's Heritage Coast booklet: "Sands
-end Trail".   Part of the route takes you up the south side
of Deepgrove Quarry, and along the edge of the fields
above. This offers superb views of the Ness, and over
Sandsend down the coast. A stile and finger-post point the
steep way down beside Gaytress Quarry to rejoin the track.

Between
Deepgrove
and the Ness
the vegetation
is only slowly
gaining a hold
on the alum wastes.

51.

Sandsend to Whitby

Sandsend Beck

• Sandsend is two small villages clustered around two parallel becks : <u>Sandsend and East Row</u>. Between them has grown up the relatively modern seafront with its hotels and Edwardian frontages, quite different from the rustic feel of the original cottages and inn. The crowds pass Sandsend by, on their way to or from Whitby, but here is the finest beach between Saltburn and Scarborough, with relative quiet to enjoy it.

• Inland from East Row bridge, well-behaved visitors may be able to visit <u>Mulgrave Woods</u>. These are private, but the good paths may be open on Wednesdays, Saturdays and Sundays (except in May). Old castles, and the charming woodlands, will make a change!

East Row: the Hart Inn

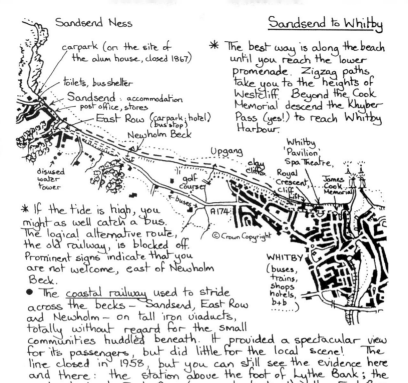

Sandsend Ness

carpark (on the site of the alum house, closed 1867)

toilets, bus shelter

Sandsend : accommodation post office, stores

East Row (carpark; hotel) (bus stop)

Newholm Beck

disused water tower

golf course

← buses

A174

© Crown Copyright

Upgang

clay cliffs

Whitby 'Pavilion' Spa Theatre,

Royal Crescent, Cliff

James Cook Memorial

WHITBY (buses, trains, shops hotels, b+b ......)

* The best way is along the beach until you reach the lower promenade. Zigzag paths take you to the heights of Westcliff. Beyond the Cook Memorial descend the Khyber Pass (yes!) to reach Whitby Harbour.

* If the tide is high, you might as well catch a bus. The logical alternative route, the old railway, is blocked off. Prominent signs indicate that you are not welcome, east of Newholm Beck.

• The <u>coastal railway</u> used to stride across the becks — Sandsend, East Row and Newholm — on tall iron viaducts, totally without regard for the small communities huddled beneath. It provided a spectacular view for its passengers, but did little for the local scene! The line closed in 1958, but you can still see the evidence here and there: the station above the foot of Lythe Bank; the goods shed at East Row (now a boat store!); the East Row bypass along the formation; the abutments of Newholm Beck viaduct; and the unwelcoming cutting through the golf course.

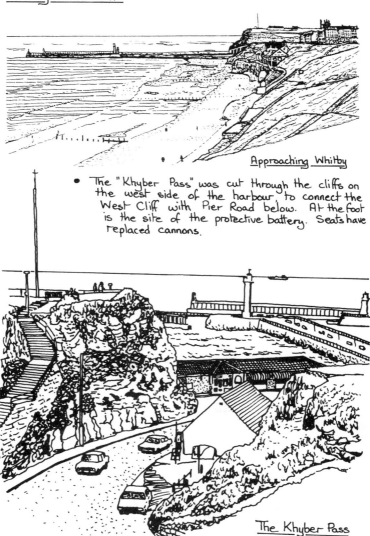

Approaching Whitby

- The "Khyber Pass" was cut through the cliffs on the west side of the harbour, to connect the West Cliff with Pier Road below. At the foot is the site of the protective battery. Seats have replaced cannons.

The Khyber Pass

● Those who have read of Whitby's haphazard charm, of its little back-alleys and pantiled houses clustered steeply up the river banks, will wonder if this can possibly be the right town, if they arrive from the west. Here, on the West Cliff, is space and order, with tall Victorian terraces more like Newcastle than a fishing village. These were the inspiration of George Hudson, the "Railway King", who realised Whitby's possibilities as a resort once

the steam railway had arrived from York in 1847. Land on the western heights was bought and carefully laid out in the then fashionable style. As well as houses there are gardens, promenades (and shelters!), with terraced walks down to the beach. Down below is the Pavilion, built for genteel entertainment and refreshment, with the Spa Theatre next door. For those without the energy to climb the cliffs, there is even a vertical lift.

55.   The Royal Crescent

Whitby Harbour

Whitby is a remarkable town, full of history, traditions, charm and good sound sense. Cut off by fearsome gradients on the landward side, it is a town of the sea. James Cook, the great explorer, is a good example of its sea-faring traditions.

The <u>Whale's Jaw Bone</u> (left) is a reminder that Whitby was once a centre for the whaling industry. (Indeed, the town's gas supply was made from whale oil.) It must have been a rough, tough town then! But the whaling industry came to a stop, as did the herring industry more recently. The fishing boats of the North Sea still call on their travels, but in smaller numbers. Whitby has its own fleet of about 80 boats:- keel boats, cobles and salmon cobles. There are also small boats for sea-anglers. Now there is a growth in leisure-boating, and the port has a marina and all that is needed to support small boats. Ships too have been seen again in Whitby (since 1958) with about 140 thousand tonnes of imports and 30000 tonnes of exports each year.

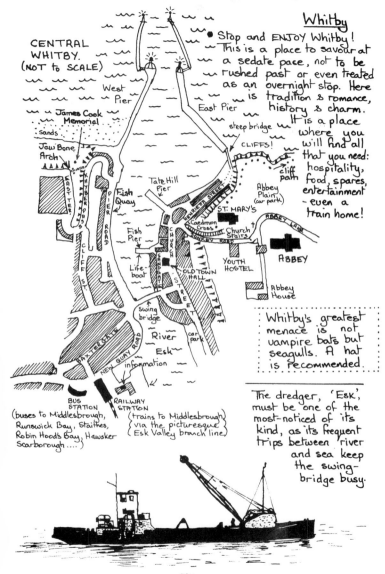

Whitby

CENTRAL WHITBY. (NOT to SCALE)

● Stop and ENJOY Whitby! This is a place to savour at a sedate pace, not to be rushed past or even treated as an overnight stop. Here is tradition & romance, history & charm. It is a place where you will find all that you need: hospitality, food, spares, entertainment - even a train home!

West Pier

East Pier

James Cook Memorial

Sands

Jaw Bone Arch

steep bridge

CLIFFS!

cliff path

Abbey Plain (car park)

EAST PIER

WHITBY SANDS

PIER ROAD

Fish Quay

Tate Hill Pier

HENRIETTA STREET

ST. MARY'S

Caedmon Cross

Church Stairs

ABBEY LANE

CLIFF ST

Fish Pier

CHURCH STREET

DONKEY ROAD

ABBEY

Lifeboat

SANDGATE

OLD TOWN HALL

YOUTH HOSTEL

Abbey House

BAXTERGATE

Swing bridge

NEW QUAY ROAD

River Esk

car park

information

BUS STATION

RAILWAY STATION

(buses to Middlesbrough, Runswick Bay, Staithes, Robin Hood's Bay, Hawsker Scarborough ....)

(trains to Middlesbrough) {via the picturesque} {Esk Valley branch line}

> Whitby's greatest menace is not vampire bats but seagulls. A hat is recommended.

The dredger, 'Esk', must be one of the most-noticed of its kind, as its frequent trips between river and sea keep the swing-bridge busy.

Whitby : East Town

• Beyond the swing-bridge,
on the east bank of the river,
the old town of Whitby nestles
below the Abbey and the Church.
<u>Sandgate</u> or <u>Church Street</u>
alike will lead you to the
Old Town Hall.
  Both streets are narrow
and full of little shops
selling everything from
real Whitby jet to Hong-
Kong plastic spiders, local
fish to Turkish Delight.
• The <u>Old Town Hall</u> (right)
stands at the top of the
Market Place. A large
upper room was used for
meetings. It was built in
1788 at the order of
Nathaniel Cholmley, whose
family had bought Whitby
from Henry VIII after the
Dissolution of the Monasteries
in 1540.

• The pattern of the town is set by
its cramped location between river and
cliff. As more houses became needed
than could front onto Church Street,
they had to be built behind, with access
via the yards (or ghauts). Should you
be tempted to explore, remember that
people live here, and respect their
privacy!
• The red pantiles were brought as ballast
by empty sailing vessels returning from
the Netherlands.

58.

● Alleys give access to the river-front. Below the Market Place you can reach the <u>Fish Pier</u>, where the 18th century fish market was held. Now the modern lifeboat is berthed here. Below Church Stairs you can get through onto <u>Tate Hill Pier</u>.

● Beyond Church Stairs the lane continues as <u>Henrietta Street</u> (named after Nathaniel Cholmley's wife in 1761, but existing, as Haggerlythe, for many centuries before). Many houses were destroyed here by cliff-falls in 1787 and 1871. Now it comes to a messy end just before the bridge onto the East Pier. Still the smell and smoke of kipper-curing will be found here.

Henrietta Street

Whitby : the piers

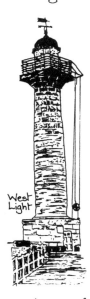

West Light

• The piers at Whitby are worth a visit. The West Pier can be easily reached from the foot of the Khyber Pass. The East Pier is rather more of an adventure. Go along Henrietta Street (beyond the foot of Church Stairs). A spindly bridge (slippery when wet) leads steeply down onto the end of the massive pier.

Here is an exciting place to be when waves roll in from the North Sea to crash against the towering cliffs and gush through the gap between the pier and the cliffs. It can also be a dangerous place when the seas are large — the pier has no handrails!

Clever design means that waves seldom enter the main harbour. Unless they come from between north-west and north-east, they just batter against the massive piers. Between these compass points, they can enter the mouth of the harbour, but the curved outer piers deflect them through the gaps to the outside of the main piers! Ingenious!

There have been sea-piers at Whitby since at least the 16th century. The East Pier was rebuilt in stone in about 1702, the West Pier in 1814.

East Light

West Pier at sunset

- The West Pier Lighthouse was built in 1831. It is 83 feet (25 m) high. A black ball is raised to indicate that large vessels may safely enter. It has a green light.
- The East Pier Lighthouse is shorter, at 54 feet (16 m). It was built in 1854.
- The "Daleks" are not escapees from Dr. Who, but old capstans. Note the ratchets at their base, and the pulleys nearby on the edges of the piers.
- The outer beacons (Green - West, Red - East) may be reached by the walkways above the outer branches of the piers. The view of Whitby from here is superb!

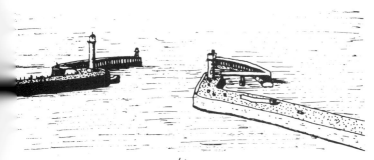

- <u>Church Stairs</u> have been in existence for a very long time: they were mentioned in 1370. They were made of wood at that time. In 1702 a start was made on replacing them with the stone staircase.

If you hear people muttering quietly to themselves as you go up or down, it is not because visitors to Whitby Abbey are incurably insane — they are just reassuring themselves that no-one has removed any of the 199 steps. If you find the climb hard work, remember to pause to enjoy the view, and be thankful that you are not carrying a coffin up to the clifftop graveyard!

Beside the steps is the Donkey Road, the old public road to the Abbey and on to Hawsker. It is just as steep as the stairs!

- <u>St Mary's Churchyard</u> surrounds the church at the top of the stairs. As one stands here on an evening, with the shadows of the gravestones lengthening on the bleak clifftop, one can quite see why Bram Stoker chose this as a location for his Dracula story.

But in the midst of the yard St Mary's has a much better story to tell about the resurrection of the dead!

- <u>Caedmon's Cross</u>, at the head of the stairs, commemorates the untutored Saxon herdsman who suddenly discovered that he had a gift of poetry and song in praise of God. He became a monk in the Abbey during the time of Hilda, in the 7th century. The cross dates from 1898.

Saint Mary's Church, Whitby.

- St. Mary's is one of the most interesting church buildings in Northern England, with many unusual features.

The present structure was begun in Norman times, about 1100 AD, probably on the site of a wooden Saxon church. The nave followed soon after, and the <u>tower</u> in 1170. North and South transepts were added in 1225 and 1380, giving a cruciform church.

- The Lord of the Manor's Pew, most unusually right across the chancel arch where the old rood-screen would have been, was erected by the Cholmleys between 1600 and 1625. This is still there, making the chancel dark and secluded.

- <u>Galleries</u> were added in other parts of the church, built between 1697 and 1764, followed by their unusual
- <u>external staircases</u>.

The nave was extended in 1819 to its present large rectangular form, and the galleries revised. To help pay for the extension there was a public auction of the <u>box pews</u>. These too remain today, with various degrees of upholstery.

Other things to note:
* The unusual large rectangular windows that brighten the interior.
* The roof sky-lights, following ship-board practice.
* The very plain Communion Table is considered to be one of the earliest following Reformation orders to replace stone altars by wooden tables. It is probably Elizabethan.
* The tall pulpit in the centre of the church, resembling a ship's crows-nest.
* The early Victorian hearing aid, for the benefit of the Minister's wife
* The large wooden tablets bearing the Ten Commandments. Elizabeth decreed that such should replace effigies and paintings.
* The chandelier (1769)
* The parish chest may be 15th century. It has three locks, one each for Minister and church-wardens. It survived being thrown over the cliff during a robbery in 1743!
* Two royal coats-of-arms: one from 1764, with the French fleur-de-lys and the horse of Hanover; and one Victorian.

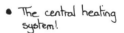

* The central heating system!

* The Scoresby Chair, commemorating Whitby's Master Mariner, scientist and explorer, Rev. Dr. William Scoresby. The chair is carved from the remains of the "Royal Charter", one of his survey vessels.

Saint Mary's, interior, with box pews, pulpit, the coat of arms, Cholmley Pew, central heating, galleries........

Whitby Abbey

- This is one of the great places in the history of Christianity in Britain. A double monastery of monks and nuns was set up here in AD 657 by Hilda, who had been abbess of Hartlepool. A pupil of Rome's first missionary to the North, Paulinus, she was a strict abbess, and Whitby's reputation grew. It was to a synod at Whitby in 664 that the church brought its early differences. The Celtic traditions, introduced through Iona & Lindisfarne were clashing with Roman practices that had come via Canterbury. King Oswy of Northumbria ruled in favour of Canterbury (their archbishop still takes precedence over York), so that, amongst other things, we adopted the Roman method of determining Easter (the first Sunday after the full moon after the spring equinox, if you've forgotten!)

The monastery lasted 200 years, then was destroyed by the Danish invasion of 867 AD.

After another 200 years the ruins appealed so strongly to Reinfrid (one of William's Norman knights) that he became a monk and set up a new Abbey. His monks built a church in the grand Norman style, that was extended and renewed over three hundred years. Whitby Abbey prospered with gifts, but the cost of the church gradually reduced it to penury. The standards among the monks lapsed too, and the Abbey was persuaded to "volunteer" closure in Henry VIII's Dissolution of Abbeys in 1549.

After the Dissolution the Abbey was sold to the Cholmley family, who used the stone from the domestic quarters for their own buildings (including Abbey House). The church, stripped of its roof, decayed slowly. The central tower collapsed in 1830, and the Imperial German Navy inflicted some damage in 1914, with shells from the battlecruiser 'Derflinger'. Since 1920 it has been in the hands of the government, and is now managed by 'English Heritage'. It is open to the public for a small fee.

<u>Whitby Abbey to the Lighthouse.</u>

• The cliff-path east of Whitby occasionally offers a sight that is rare on the East coast of England — the sun setting over the sea, on summer evenings.

<u>Saltwick Nab</u>

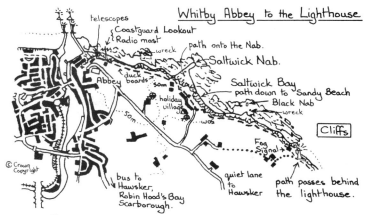

Whitby Abbey to the Lighthouse

telescopes
Coastguard Lookout
Radio mast
wreck
path onto the Nab.
Saltwick Nab.
Abbey
duck boards
50m
Saltwick Bay
path down to Sandy Beach
Black Nab
wreck
holiday village
50m
Cliffs
W6S
Fog Signal
© Crown Copyright
bus to
Hawsker,
Robin Hood's Bay
Scarborough.
quiet lane
to
Hawsker
path passes behind
the lighthouse.

* The clifftop path can be rejoined past St Mary's, along the
edge of the Abbey Plain, overlooking the harbour mouth.
The coastguard lookout is superbly situated — of course —
so make use of their judgement and survey the scene from here.
The cliff face itself is visible at times as you hug its edge
along to Saltwick Nab. This promontory is the scene
of many shipwrecks and some heroic rescues. Now it is
in the care of the National Trust.
The path follows Cleveland Way signs through the caravan
park, rejoining the cliff edge at the top of the zig-zag
path down to Saltwick Bay. Follow the cliffs onwards,
past the Fog Signal.

Whitby Light

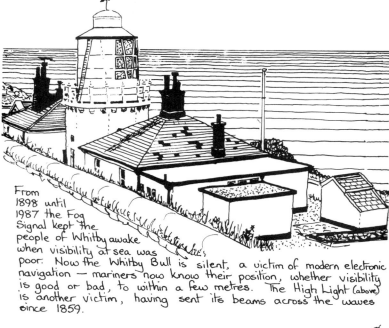

From 1898 until 1987 the Fog Signal kept the people of Whitby awake when visibility at sea was poor. Now the Whitby Bull is silent, a victim of modern electronic navigation — mariners now know their position, whether visibility is good or bad, to within a few metres. The High Light (above) is another victim, having sent its beams across the waves since 1859.

Maw Wyke Hole
↓

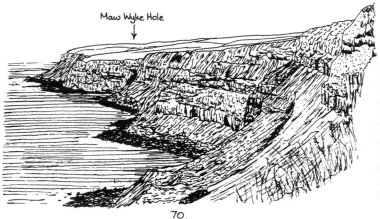

* The path from the Fog Signal station goes up to a stile just by the gate of the lighthouse. On the other side of the access road a step leads to the public path outside the wall. Go along above the lighthouse, and slant up the field beyond to a stile.

Now the path marches along the undulating cliff edge, sometimes inside the fence, at others outside.

Along here you will meet blasted thorn-bushes, bent by the furious winds from the sea.

Two dips to cross becks, are followed by muddy climbs up steep banks.

Maw Wyke Hole is the third depression. Positive identification is provided by the overlooking caravans of Northcliffe Caravan Park! (Hawsker is just up the path and lane, for those who have had enough!)

• Between here and Robin Hood's Bay you share the coast not only with Cleveland Way walkers, but also those who have followed Wainwright's Coast to Coast route from St Bee's in Cumbria.

View north from Maw Wyke Hole.

71.

Homerell Hole
and Craze Naze.

- Here, as in many other places along this coastline, the various
  strata underlying the land are exposed. The variety of
  thin seams is very obvious, and is enough to give even the
  uninitiated a desire to know more geology.

72.

Maw Wyke Hole to Robin Hood's Bay

Maw Wyke Hole

a steep zigzag path goes down the cliff-face to the beach. It is NOT our route, and not for the faint-hearted!

bus to Whitby

Oakham Beck

Coast to Coast

High Hawsker

Crown Copyright

wool

disused railway (path)

Bottom House

bus

White Stone Hole

High Scar

Clock Case Nab

Craze Naze

Homerell Hole

link path

wosi

Cliffs!

fields

Coast Guard lookout

Ness Point
(National Trust)

170m
Smails Moor Farm
150m

100m

wreck

Rocket Post Field: these seats are at the best viewpoints.

← bus →

large car park

bus to ← Scarborough

car park toilets

steep bank

abandoned section of road (and replacement)

Robin Hood's Bay.

* From the bridge over Oakham Beck climb up again round the rim of Maw Wyke Hole. Continue your clifftop progress, with a succession of rises and dips. In places there are spectacular views of the cliffs. It is safe in daylight, but if caught by dusk you should retire to the old railway line.

As you round Ness Point the Peak at Ravenscar comes into view, but the town of Robin Hood's Bay stays quite hidden until you reach Rocket Post Field. Watch for the exit from the field, hidden in a thicket. Go carefully between houses and their gardens into the village.

Robin Hood's Bay

The older part of Bay village — the interesting part for the visitor — lies down the slope, below the carparks. Cars of non-residents are not allowed down, for reasons that become obvious as you penetrate its narrow steep streets and maze of alleyways.

It is worth taking time to explore, returning another day if necessary. From Bay Bank little alleys entice

you to wander. The houses cluster closely, but the alleys are interconnected by steps and openings, giving a multiplicity of routes down to the foot of the Town.

King's Beck cuts a deep gash down the centre of the village, an unexpected breath of green amidst the tightly-packed houses. Further down, the beck has been covered over to provide extra building space. It emerges by the <u>Bay Hotel</u>, below the Dock, to splash onto the beach.

New Road is the main way now up from the Dock. The older way is King Street (left) which comes to an abrupt end where it slipped into the sea (along with a sizeable chunk of the village) in 1780. The steady erosion of the village (about 200 cottages in 200 years) was slowed by the erection of the massive sea-wall in 1975. Even so, the Bay Hotel and the Marine Laboratory, flanking the Dock, take a tremendous <u>battering</u> when the wind blows from the wrong quarter. The Bay Hotel has even had a ship wrecked against it in 1893, when the brig Romulus tried to come in through a window, bowsprit first!

Despite the lack of a harbour, or even much space to pull boats clear of the surf, this was primarily a fishing village, with its own lifeboat that operated from the station on the Dock. It was villages like this that produced the mariners who would first circumnavigate the world and spread the red colour of the British Empire around the globe.

Robin Hood's Bay was also a successful smuggling centre with its maze of alleys and interconnecting houses. It is said that many houses had openings into the covered way of King's Beck, so that contraband could more easily avoid the clutches of the King's Men. Tea as well as spirits formed the inward trade, balanced by a flow of Yorkshire wool, carried over the Moors by pony.

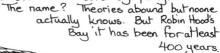

The name? Theories abound but noone actually knows. But Robin Hood's Bay it has been for at least 400 years.

From the south.

- The youth hostel at Boggle Hole was once a mill, with access by ship to the wharf at high tide. 'Boggle' or 'bogle' is the local term for a hobgoblin. This delightful little valley, closed by the sea, seems a superb place for such a one to live.

Robin Hood's Bay to Boggle Hole

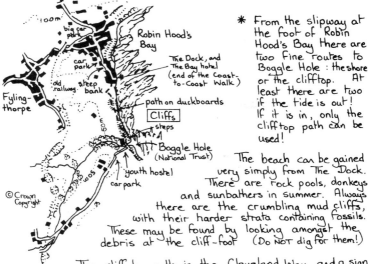

* From the slipway at the foot of Robin Hood's Bay there are two fine routes to Boggle Hole: the shore or the clifftop. At least there are two if the tide is out! If it is in, only the clifftop path can be used!

The beach can be gained very simply from The Dock. There are rock pools, donkeys and sunbathers in summer. Always there are the crumbling mud cliffs, with their harder strata containing fossils. These may be found by looking amongst the debris at the cliff-foot (Do NOT dig for them!)

The cliff-top path is the Cleveland Way, and a sign in Albion Street points the steep way up past the red roofs onto the clifftop. Some parts have subsided, and duck-boards are used. Don't forget to look back over the roofs! The path eventually disappears into a heap of thorn-bushes, where you descend steeply into Boggle Hole.

Boggle Hole with the tide in.

* From the bridge over Mill Beck you can climb up steeply (NOT the lane!) to regain the cliff path. along to Stoupe Beck. Alternatively you can follow the beach if the tide is out.

Beyond Stoupe Beck bridge a lane goes steeply up under the trees. It is a deep quagmire! Fortunately there is a stepped pavement with a handrail (it can still be slippery on a wet day). Go up past the farm and along the road to a bend. A Cleveland Way sign points the way back to the cliff-edge for 800m or so. There are fine views to Ravenscar, and down to Flat Scars when the tide is out. The path then turns briefly uphill, then contours along towards Ravenscar across the fields. At a wood it turns steeply uphill again, levelling out beside the old railway. Walk along to Ravenscar, climbing up to meet the road at the National Trust information centre.

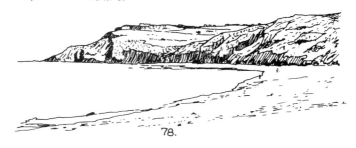

Boggle Hole to Ravenscar

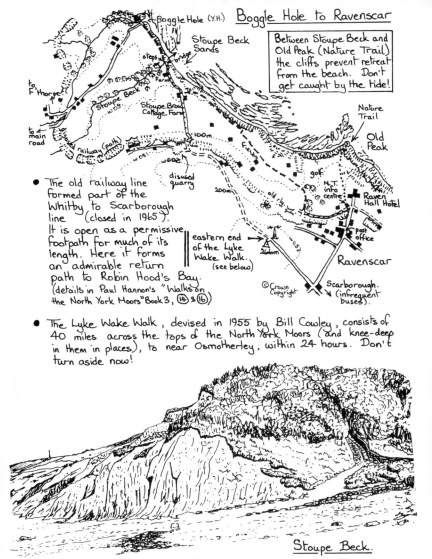

Between Stoupe Beck and Old Peak (Nature Trail) the cliffs prevent retreat from the beach. Don't get caught by the tide!

- The old railway line formed part of the Whitby to Scarborough line (closed in 1965). It is open as a permissive footpath for much of its length. Here it forms an admirable return path to Robin Hood's Bay. (details in Paul Hannon's "Walks on the North York Moors" Book 3, ⑭ & ⑯)

eastern end of the Lyke Wake Walk. (see below)

© Crown Copyright

- The Lyke Wake Walk, devised in 1955 by Bill Cowley, consists of 40 miles across the tops of the North York Moors (and knee-deep in them in places), to near Osmotherley, within 24 hours. Don't turn aside now!

Stoupe Beck.

79.

Ravenscar

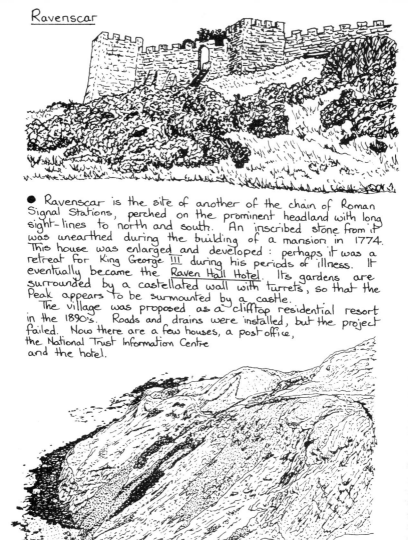

● Ravenscar is the site of another of the chain of Roman Signal Stations, perched on the prominent headland with long sight-lines to north and south. An inscribed stone from it was unearthed during the building of a mansion in 1774. This house was enlarged and developed: perhaps it was a retreat for King George III during his periods of illness. It eventually became the Raven Hall Hotel. Its gardens are surrounded by a castellated wall with turrets, so that the Peak appears to be surmounted by a castle.

The village was proposed as a clifftop residential resort in the 1890's. Roads and drains were installed, but the project failed. Now there are a few houses, a post office, the National Trust Information Centre and the hotel.

✱ Next to the hotel entrance a path goes down across the golf course towards the shore. Below the fairways it descends quite steeply, partly in an unexpected furrow. This is the line of the <u>Peak Fault</u>. 35 million years ago there was a dramatic upheaval here, with part of the land being lifted up by 150 metres and carried inland some distance. So the rocks south-east of the path are much younger than those to the north-west, coinciding with those exposed in the quarry up near the old railway. See if you can see any difference! The path continues down to the shore, where it is easy to find ammonites. But please do not dig them out of the rocks: there are plenty amongst the beach debris. You may also find various pieces of wreckage: this is a spot notorious for its wrecks.

Return to the hilltop by the same path, unless the tide is right and you have time and inclination to walk along to the next beach access – Stoupe Beck.

(The "Ravenscar Geological Trail" – a North York Moors National Park booklet – is a useful guide).

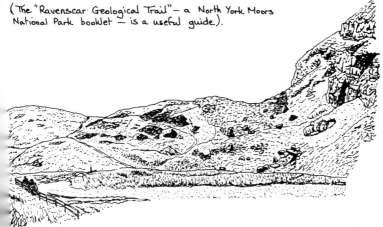

● The <u>Peak Fault</u> is responsible for an abrupt change in the coastal scenery. North of Ravenscar the rocks at sea-level are a succession of Lias rocks. Their frequent changes of hardness give a series of bays (soft rocks at sea-level) and headlands (harder rocks). South of the Fault the sea-level rocks tend to be the much more uniform Deltaic series, so the coast is straighter, with cliffs of a uniform height and fewer bays.

- <u>Common Cliff</u> (above) and <u>Beast Cliff</u> (below), both have a wide
undercliff, an extensive ledge 50 metres above the sea. The
northern end has several pools, and the southern is covered
with a rich carpet of trees. It is remarkably difficult to reach,
despite the indications of rights of way on the 1:50 000 O.S.
maps. Although I have looked carefully I have failed to find
any reasonable path down the rim of crags that jealously
guard this beautiful area.

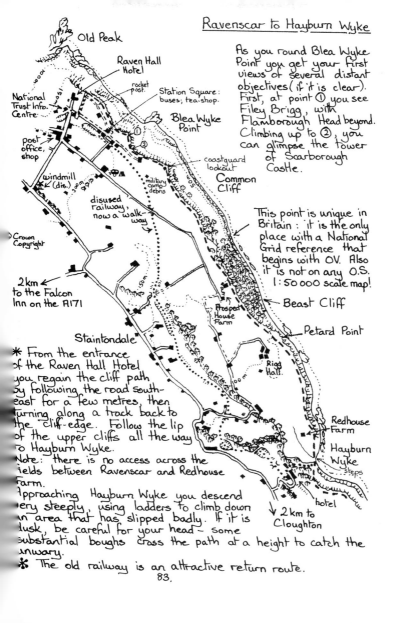

Ravenscar to Hayburn Wyke

Old Peak

Raven Hall Hotel

rocket post.

Station Square: buses; tea-shop.

National Trust Info. Centre

Blea Wyke Point

post office, shop

coastguard lookout

windmill (dis.)

military camp debris

Common Cliff

disused railway, now a walk-way

) Crown Copyright

2km to the Falcon Inn on the A171

Beast Cliff

Petard Point

Prospect House Farm

Staintondale

Rigg Hall

Redhouse Farm

Hayburn Wyke steps

hotel

↓ 2km to Cloughton

As you round Blea Wyke Point you get your first views of several distant objectives (if it is clear). First, at point ① you see Filey Brigg, with Flamborough Head beyond. Climbing up to ②, you can glimpse the tower of Scarborough Castle.

This point is unique in Britain: it is the only place with a National Grid reference that begins with OV. Also it is not on any O.S. 1:50 000 scale map!

✻ From the entrance of the Raven Hall Hotel you regain the cliff path by following the road south-east for a few metres, then turning along a track back to the cliff-edge. Follow the lip of the upper cliffs all the way to Hayburn Wyke.
Note: there is no access across the fields between Ravenscar and Redhouse Farm.
Approaching Hayburn Wyke you descend very steeply, using ladders to climb down an area that has slipped badly. If it is dusk, be careful for your head — some substantial boughs cross the path at a height to catch the unwary.
✻ The old railway is an attractive return route.

Hayburn Wyke

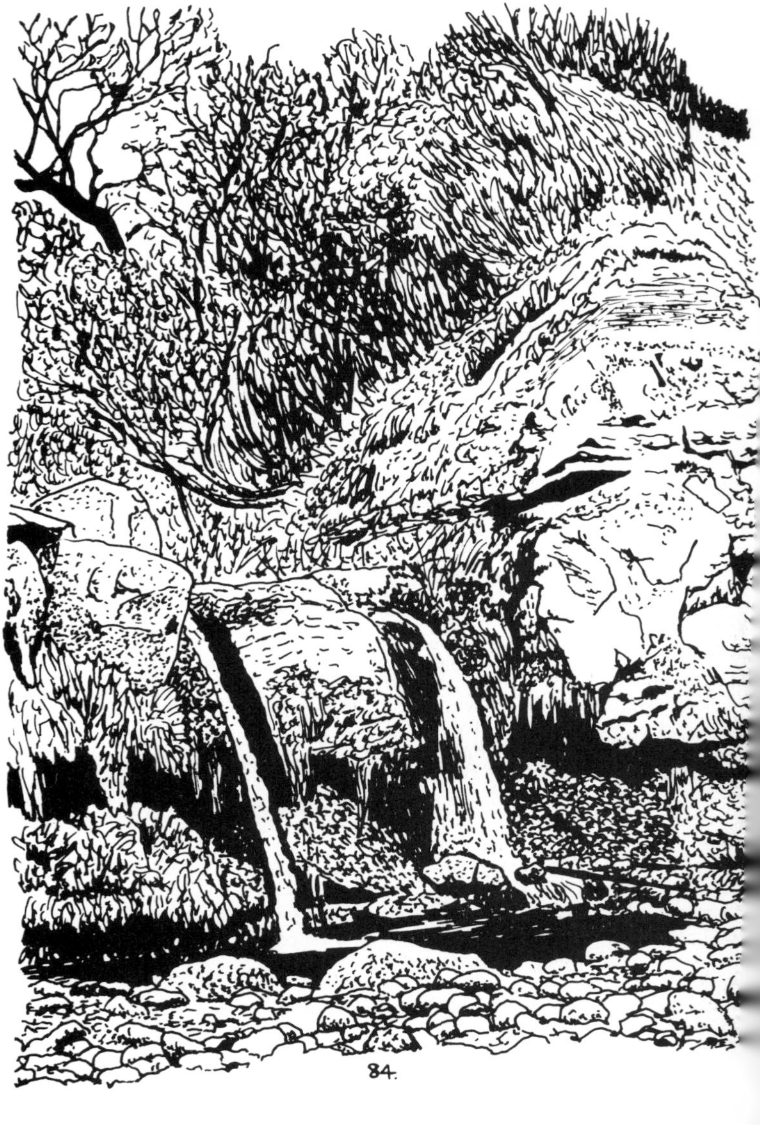

Hayburn Wyke

Hayburn Wyke is something different on this coastline of cliffs. Here Hayburn Beck tumbles down to the sea, cutting a deep nick, and finally gushes over twin waterfalls to disappear in a beach of rounded boulders. The valley is beautifully wooded. It is a Nature Reserve, in the care of Yorkshire Naturalist's Trust and the National Trust. The woodlands have well laid-out paths which allow almost anyone to enjoy their charm. A hotel, with a carpark, lies at the top of the wood.

View from the seat on the south side of the Wyke.

Hayburn Wyke to Cloughton Wyke.

The Undercliff, seen from the seat on the way up from the beach.

* From the beach a path climbs up through the luxuriant growth of the wood (including invasive rhododendrons). A seat perched on the cliff-edge gives great views both ways. Further up, our path, clearly labelled "Cleveland Way", leaves the main path, turning left. (The other path goes up through the woods to the hotel.) Follow the Way up onto the higher clifftop, and follow the old coastguard path along the top, climbing to 112 metres above sea-level. Below you is the lush wood of the Undercliff, rich in wild-life but not a route for a walker with a sense of survival! Much of the top cliff is edged with thorn-bushes, which block much of the seaward view. There is gorse too. But then there is a spell on the very edge of vertical cliffs, then a set of steps leads you down through the end of a wood. Note how the beach rocks now show the pavement style of limestone. Keep on along the path, up and down, to reach Cloughton Wyke (A tarmac road leads inland to Cloughton).

The old station at Hayburn Wyke.

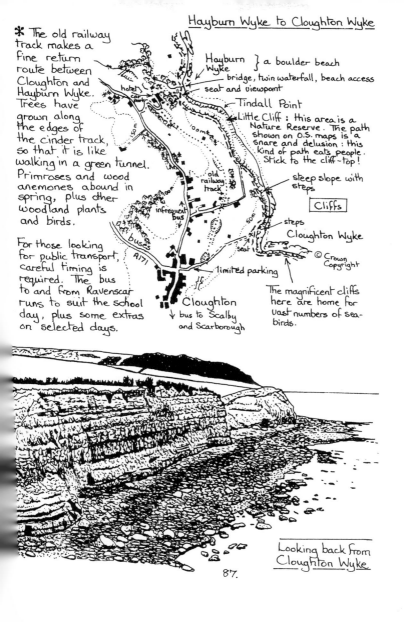

Hayburn Wyke to Cloughton Wyke

* The old railway track makes a fine return route between Cloughton and Hayburn Wyke. Trees have grown along the edges of the cinder track, so that it is like walking in a green tunnel. Primroses and wood anemones abound in spring, plus other woodland plants and birds.

For those looking for public transport, careful timing is required. The bus to and from Ravenscar runs to suit the school day, plus some extras on selected days.

Hayburn Wyke } a boulder beach

bridge, twin waterfall, beach access

seat and viewpoint

Tindall Point

Little Cliff : this area is a Nature Reserve. The path shown on O.S. maps is a snare and delusion : this kind of path eats people. Stick to the cliff-top!

steep slope with steps

Cliffs

steps

Cloughton Wyke

© Crown Copyright

hotel

car

old railway track

infrequent bus

buses

A171

limited parking

Cloughton
↓ bus to Scalby and Scarborough

The magnificent cliffs here are home for vast numbers of sea-birds.

Looking back from Cloughton Wyke

87.

Cloughton Wyke to Scalby Mills

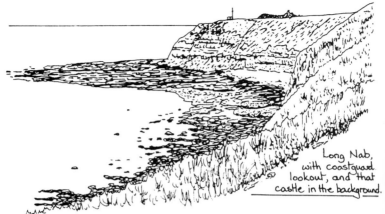

Long Nab,
with coastguard
lookout, and that
castle in the background.

● The rocky beaches and cliffs show part of the Middle Deltaic Series of sandstones and shales, all topped with clay from the Ice Ages. It seems strange to think that this rock was being formed as sediments on riverbeds and seabeds at the time that dinosaurs were around. Large footprints, (up to 60cm) have been found in Burniston Wyke, and plant fossils can be found near Scalby Ness and Cloughton Wyke.

Scalby Beck

Cloughton Wyke to Scalby Mills.

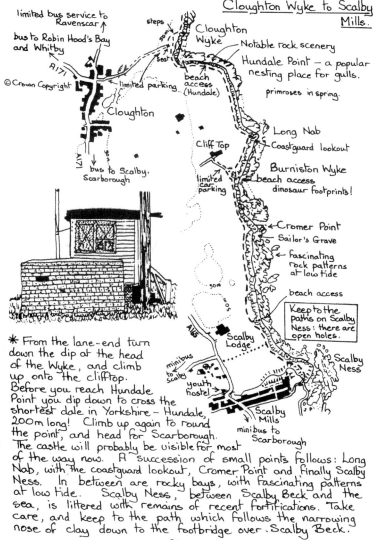

limited bus service to Ravenscar ↑

bus to Robin Hood's Bay and Whitby

A171

© Crown Copyright

steps

Cloughton Wyke

Notable rock scenery

Hundale Point – a popular nesting place for gulls.

primroses in spring.

Seat

beach access (Hundale)

limited parking

Cloughton

A171

bus to Scalby, Scarborough

Cliff Top

Long Nab
Coastguard lookout

Burniston Wyke
beach access
dinosaur footprints!

limited car parking

Cromer Point
Sailor's Grave

fascinating rock patterns at low tide

beach access

Keep to the paths on Scalby Ness: there are open holes.

A165

Scalby Lodge

minibus to Scalby

youth hostel

Scalby Ness

Scalby Mills
minibus to Scarborough

✳ From the lane-end turn down the dip at the head of the Wyke, and climb up onto the clifftop. Before you reach Hundale Point you dip down to cross the shortest dale in Yorkshire – Hundale, 200m long! Climb up again to round the point, and head for Scarborough. The castle will probably be visible for most of the way now. A succession of small points follows: Long Nab, with the coastguard lookout, Cromer Point and finally Scalby Ness. In between are rocky bays, with fascinating patterns at low tide. Scalby Ness, between Scalby Beck and the sea, is littered with remains of recent fortifications. Take care, and keep to the path which follows the narrowing nose of clay down to the footbridge over Scalby Beck.

89.

● The <u>Marine Drive</u> round Scarborough's headland, linking North and South Bays, is a recent addition. It was begun in 1897 and completed in 1908 (at a cost of £122 008). A new seawall had to be built below the castle cliffs. Tolls were levied until 1950. It certainly makes a very different way to reach the South Bay compared with crossing the ridge through the town.

In bad weather it can be dangerous, and is then closed to all traffic (including pedestrians).

North Bay cliff lift.

Scalby Mills to Scarborough.

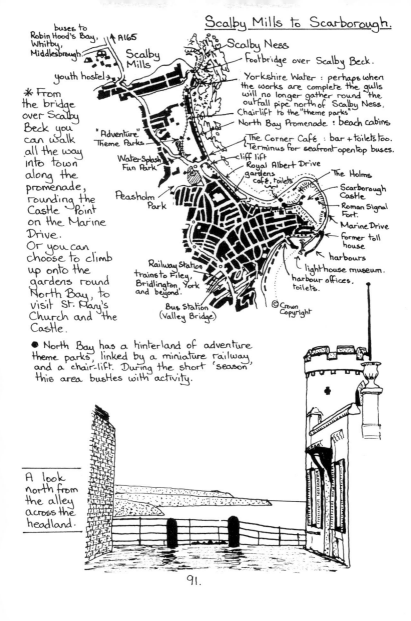

buses to Robin Hood's Bay, Whitby, Middlesbrough.

↑ A165

Scalby Mills

youth hostel

Scalby Ness

Footbridge over Scalby Beck.

Yorkshire Water : perhaps when the works are complete the gulls will no longer gather round the outfall pipe north of Scalby Ness.

Chairlift to the "theme parks"

North Bay Promenade : beach cabins

"Adventure" Theme Parks

Water Splash Fun Park

The Corner Café : bar + toilets too.
Terminus for seafront opentop buses.

cliff lift

Royal Albert Drive gardens café, toilets.

The Holms

Peasholm Park

Scarborough Castle

Roman Signal Fort.

Marine Drive

former toll house

Railway Station trains to Filey, Bridlington, York and beyond.

harbours

lighthouse museum.

harbour offices. toilets.

Bus Station (Valley Bridge)

© Crown Copyright

* From the bridge over Scalby Beck you can walk all the way into town along the promenade, rounding the Castle Point on the Marine Drive.
Or you can choose to climb up onto the gardens round North Bay, to visit St. Mary's Church and the Castle.

● North Bay has a hinterland of adventure theme parks, linked by a miniature railway and a chair-lift. During the short 'season' this area bustles with activity.

A look north from the alley across the headland.

Scarborough Castle

● Scarborough Castle is in the care of English Heritage, and may be visited on payment of the usual fee. The <u>Norman Keep</u> dominates the headland. It is this that has caught the eye all the way down the coast path from Ravenscar. It was built in the reign of Henry II, from 1158 to 1168 AD, and survived until split open by artillery in 1645 whilst besieged by an army of Scots on the Parliamentary side.

• The headland, a naturally strong position overlooking the town and harbour, was properly fortified in 1136AD, with a keep and a curtain wall. Henry II, trying to wrest power from the barons, had to besiege it in order to take it from William le Gros, Earl of Yorkshire. Henry had the Great Keep built, and added further defences. But it was difficult and expensive to maintain, and a succession of sieges during the next few hundred years did little to conserve it!

The advent of <u>artillery</u> made most 'keep and curtain' castles redundant, as the thin walls were readily and cheaply reduced by the new cannons. But Scarborough Castle's position high on the headland allowed it to survive into the age of the gun, and it played a prominent part in the English Civil Wars between 1642 and 1649.

Several times it changed hands, or its defenders changed sides, so it was besieged persistently and was gradually knocked into ruin. In 1649 Parliament ordered its final demolition, but it was already so ruinous that it was not worthwhile to carry out the order!

A hundred years later the town asked for protection during the '45', and received a barracks and a gun battery to protect the harbour. This did not prevent it being raided by the American Paul Jones in 1779, during the Independence fracas. The German Navy, in 1914, also shelled the town & castle, destroying the barracks.

93.

Scarborough Castle

- The Romans recognised the importance of the headland as a coastal vantage point. Here they placed one of their chain of <u>signal stations</u>. Others were at Huntcliff, Goldsborough, Ravenscar and Filey (and perhaps elsewhere). They formed an early warning system so that inland cavalry could be deployed to deal with seaborne invasions. Built around 376, they had all been overrun by 400 AD.

  At Scarborough part of the remains are visible. A ditch forms a perimeter defence, followed by a walled courtyard. The gatehouse has been excavated. The signal tower once stood in the centre.

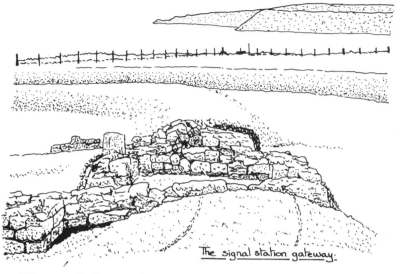

The signal station gateway.

- The site of the signal tower has been reused. The Saxons and Normans built <u>chapels</u> here, and some of these have been excavated too.

  The well within the signal station was once considered miraculous, because the water came to within 3 metres of this hilltop. (It is now dry).

  On this side the castle ends abruptly at the cliff edge, with no wall. Beyond the fence the cliffs fall to Marine Drive, which runs round the headland just above sea-level (usually!)

St. Mary's Chapel

• The Normans built the Keep and the Curtain Wall that cuts off the headland. Various towers were added to the wall at different times. A walk along the path between the Sally Port and the Barbican reveals a variety of designs & of stonework. There is even brickwork where the 1746 barracks was built.

Outside the Curtain Wall: the brick section.

Scarborough Harbours.

• The headland make South Bay a natural harbour, with protection from the north and west. Good lines of communication made it an important port for Ryedale and the Moors. A quay was constructed in the 13th century, and various piers followed. The Old Pier (now the centre one), was rebuilt and enlarged from 1732, and the East Pier was added from 1752, making two harbours. The old West piers were combined into a single structure in the 19th century. Now the East Harbour is used as a haven for pleasure craft — plus the dredger — and the West Harbour for the fishing fleet and freighters.

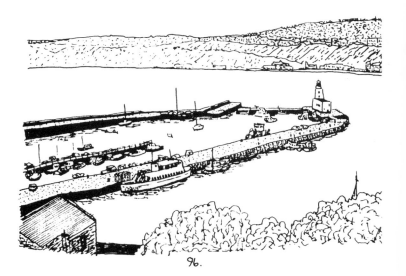

Scarborough Harbours.

- Small freighters such as the 'Hagenow' still use the port facilities, berthing alongside Sandside. Much of this traffic is to and from Scandinavia and Germany.

- Local boat trips are available during the summer season for those who want a different perspective on the coastline.

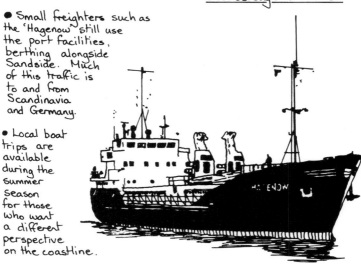

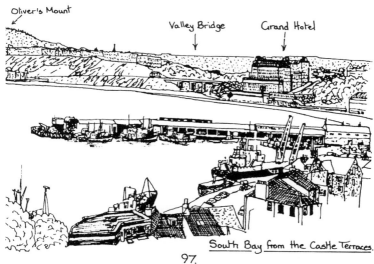

Oliver's Mount

Valley Bridge

Grand Hotel

South Bay from the Castle Terraces.

- Next door to the interesting Harbour Office on West Pier, (rather like a double-decked railway station), is the <u>Fish Market</u>. Here traders vie with each other to sell their sea-food from gaily-painted stalls. Auctions of freshly-landed fish are also held on the West Pier.

- The Old Pier terminates just beyond the <u>lighthouse</u>. This was rebuilt after the Great War, when it suffered damage by gunfire from German warships. Now it houses a museum.
A reminder of hostile times is given by the <u>gun</u> on the pier's end:

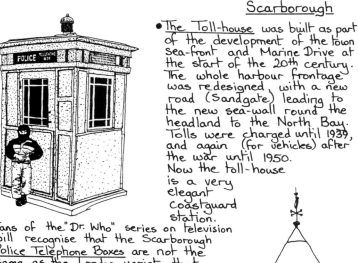

- <u>The Toll-house</u> was built as part of the development of the town sea-front and Marine Drive at the start of the 20th century. The whole harbour frontage was redesigned, with a new road (Sandgate) leading to the new sea-wall round the headland to the North Bay. Tolls were charged until 1939, and again (for vehicles) after the war until 1950. Now the toll-house is a very elegant Coastguard station.

- Fans of the "Dr. Who" series on television will recognise that the Scarborough <u>Police Telephone Boxes</u> are not the same as the London variety that achieved fame as the T.A.R.D.I.S. However, they did appear on T.V. in their own right — Scarborough was the setting for the gentle police series "Rosie".

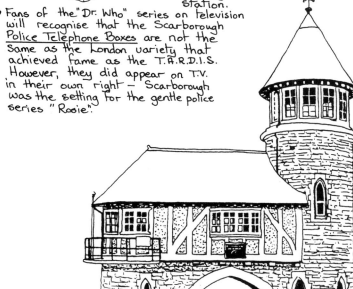

The Toll-House (Coastguard Station).

Scarborough South Bay

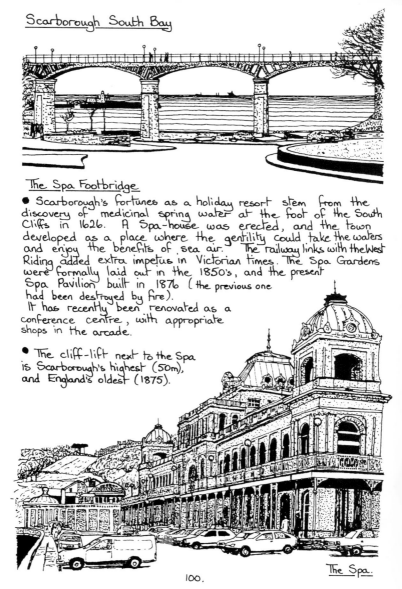

The Spa Footbridge

● Scarborough's fortunes as a holiday resort stem from the discovery of medicinal spring water at the foot of the South Cliffs in 1626. A Spa-house was erected, and the town developed as a place where the gentility could take the waters and enjoy the benefits of sea air. The railway links with the West Riding added extra impetus in Victorian times. The Spa Gardens were formally laid out in the 1850's, and the present Spa Pavilion built in 1876 (the previous one had been destroyed by fire).
It has recently been renovated as a conference centre, with appropriate shops in the arcade.

● The cliff-lift next to the Spa is Scarborough's highest (50m), and England's oldest (1875).

The Spa.

Scarborough South Bay

The Grand
Hotel (1867)

• The Esplanade, above the South Cliff
Gardens, reflects the genteel development
of the town as a resort (before the days
of day-trippers!). Here are terraces of
Victorian residences, well-cut lawns and
flower-beds. Access to the town, cut off
by the ravine of The Valley, was - and is-
made easier by the Spa footbridge (1826),
with a road-bridge performing a similar
function near the railway and bus termini.
The Valley itself is another garden, worth
a visit for its peace and quiet, despite
its central location.

• The Memorial Clock Tower
marks the limit of Victorian
Scarborough. Through its
arch you approach the wilds
again, with a view to Filey Brigg.

Scarborough to Cayton Bay.

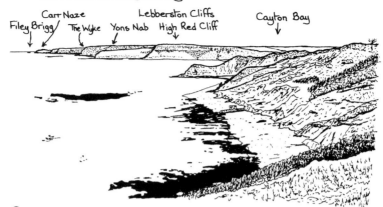

Filey Brigg   Carr Naze   Yons Nab   Lebberston Cliffs   Cayton Bay
         The Wyke   High Red Cliff

Cornelian Bay, with Osgodby Point and the cliffs to Filey Brigg.

● The path along Frank Cliff, around Cornelian Bay, gives an unusual view down onto the canopy of a wood. Here you can watch those birds that sit at the top of trees to sing — those that are usually just a dark shape against the brightness of the sky (if you can see them at all). Take binoculars with you, and a bird book.

● The woods of Osgodby (Knipe) Point are now in the care of the National Trust. They are a delight in spring and early summer, with orchids as well as the usual woodland plants: bluebells, violets, celandines, anemones, avens, ragged robin... So take your flower identification book too!

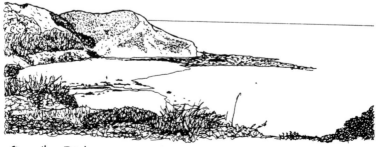

Osgodby Point.

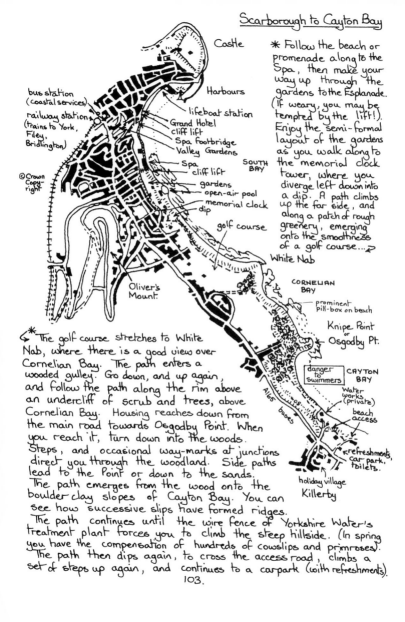

Scarborough to Cayton Bay

Castle

bus station (coastal services)

railway station (trains to York, Filey, Bridlington)

© Crown Copyright

Harbours

lifeboat station

Grand Hotel

cliff lift

Spa footbridge

Valley Gardens

Spa

cliff lift

gardens

open-air pool

memorial clock

dip

SOUTH BAY

golf course

White Nab

Oliver's Mount

CORNELIAN BAY

prominent pill-box on beach

Knipe Point or Osgodby Pt.

danger to swimmers

CAYTON BAY

Water works (private)

beach access

Alec's buses

refreshments, car park, toilets.

holiday village Killerby

* Follow the beach or promenade along to the Spa, then make your way up through the gardens to the Esplanade. (If weary, you may be tempted by the lift!). Enjoy the semi-formal layout of the gardens as you walk along to the memorial clock tower, where you diverge left down into a dip. A path climbs up the far side, and along a patch of rough greenery, emerging onto the smoothness of a golf course... ➔

⤴ * The golf course stretches to White Nab, where there is a good view over Cornelian Bay. The path enters a wooded gulley. Go down, and up again, and follow the path along the rim above an undercliff of scrub and trees, above Cornelian Bay. Housing reaches down from the main road towards Osgodby Point. When you reach it, turn down into the woods. Steps, and occasional way-marks at junctions direct you through the woodland. Side paths lead to the Point or down to the sands. The path emerges from the wood onto the boulder clay slopes of Cayton Bay. You can see how successive slips have formed ridges.

The path continues until the wire fence of Yorkshire Water's treatment plant forces you to climb the steep hillside. (In spring you have the compensation of hundreds of cowslips and primroses). The path then dips again, to cross the access road, climbs a set of steps up again, and continues to a carpark (with refreshments).

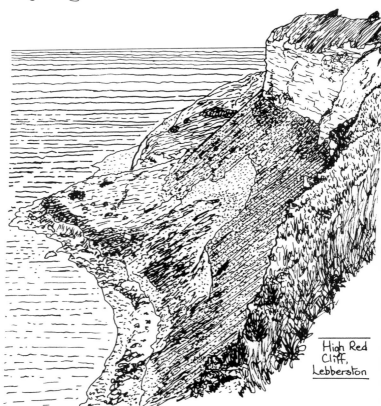

High Red
Cliff,
Lebberston

● Lebberston Cliffs striped appearance may intrigue those who
approach from the Cayton Bay side. The golden-coloured band
of vertical rock near the top of High Red Cliff is Calcareous
Grit. Below it is a much thicker layer of Oxford Clay. This
shaly clay has crumbled to give a steep grey slope partly
colonised by grass. This all sits on a base of Hackness and
Kellaways Rocks. But right next-door the much lower headland, Yons Nab has a different series: Boulder Clay tops the
Estuarine series of sandstones and limestone. A near-vertical
fault — the Red Cliff Fault — is responsible for the abrupt change.

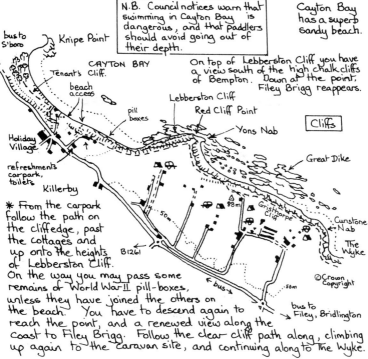

N.B. Council notices warn that swimming in Cayton Bay is dangerous, and that paddlers should avoid going out of their depth.

Cayton Bay has a superb sandy beach.

bus to S'boro

Knipe Point

CAYTON BAY

Tenant's Cliff.

beach access

pill boxes

On top of Lebberston Cliff you have a view south of the high chalk cliffs of Bempton. Down at the point, Filey Brigg reappears.

Lebberston Cliff

Red Cliff Point

Yons Nab

Cliffs

Holiday Village

refreshments carpark, toilets

Killerby

Great Dike

Gristhorpe Cliff

50m

88m

Cunstone Nab

The Wyke

B1261

© Crown Copyright

bus

50m

bus to Filey, Bridlington

* From the carpark follow the path on the cliffedge, past the cottages and up onto the heights of Lebberston Cliff. On the way you may pass some remains of World War II pill-boxes, unless they have joined the others on the beach. You have to descend again to reach the point, and a renewed view along the coast to Filey Brigg. Follow the clear cliff path along, climbing up again to the caravan site, and continuing along to The Wyke.

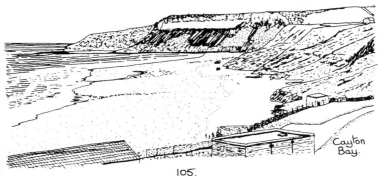

Cayton Bay.

Newbiggin Cliffs

● Filey Brigg is not a failed precursor to the Channel Tunnel. It is completely natural (apart from the buried sewer-pipe), being a layer of hard Middle Calcareous Grit, that has been worn away only slowly by the incessant action of the sea. The cliffs at the end of Carr Naze are of Osmington Oolite, capped by badly-weathered boulder clay. The Brigg is a fascinating place to explore, with its rock outcrops and pools. The waves breaking on it, sending up great gouts of spray, are visible for many miles. But be wary of their power, even at low tide, and ALWAYS keep an eye on the water level. It is too easy to get stranded.

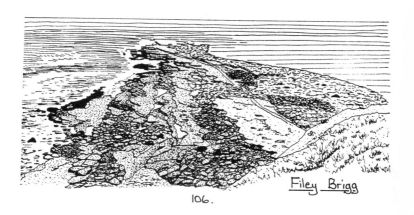

Filey Brigg

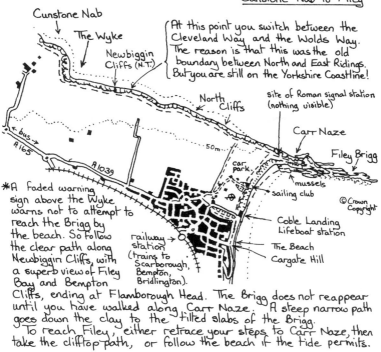

Cunstone Nab

The Wyke

Newbiggin Cliffs (N.T.)

At this point you switch between the Cleveland Way and the Wolds Way. The reason is that this was the old boundary between North and East Ridings. But you are still on the Yorkshire Coastline!

North Cliffs

site of Roman signal station (nothing visible)

Carr Naze

Filey Brigg

bus

A165

A1039

50m

carr park

mussels

sailing club

© Crown Copyright

*A faded warning sign above the Wyke warns not to attempt to reach the Brigg by the beach. So follow the clear path along Newbiggin Cliffs, with a superb view of Filey Bay and Bempton

railway station (trains to Scarborough, Bempton, Bridlington).

Coble Landing Lifeboat station

The Beach

Cargate Hill

Cliffs, ending at Flamborough Head. The Brigg does not reappear until you have walked along Carr Naze. A steep narrow path goes down the clay to the tilted slabs of the Brigg.
   To reach Filey, either retrace your steps to Carr Naze, then take the clifftop path, or follow the beach if the tide permits.

Filey Sands, from Carr Naze.

Filey

is a seaside resort with dignity. It strives hard to keep an appeal for all the family, with plenty of amenities in the town, but an absence of the worst commercial horrors. The town, sensibly, is up on the top of the low, crumbling clay cliffs, and a number of tree-lined avenues join it to The Beach — the area of gardens and promenades on top of the sea-wall. The trees and gardens are a major attractive feature of the resort.

There is a sandy beach too. It stretches all the way from the Brigg to Speeton Beach, just before the towering chalk cliffs that draw the eye round to the twin white pillars (lighthouses) on Flamborough Head. This view round Filey Bay must be one of the best in Yorkshire on a clear day.

Cargate Hill

Filey

- Filey's roots as a fishing village and haven show at the <u>Coble Landing</u>. Here the cobles and double-enders are drawn up onto the promenade above the sea-wall, or on the long ramp down to the beach. They look ready for business, their zigzag lineup reminiscent of the cars at Le Mans.

Here too is the <u>Lifeboat Station</u>, a reminder that this coast still has its storms and its hazards, even for modern shipping. The coastguards, using more modern equipment to keep track of ships, still use their eyes, too. A large window marks their new premises in the town, giving a superb view of the bay.

<u>Coble Landing and the Brigg</u>.

The woodland path to Martin's Ravine, above the Royal Parade.

South-east view from the clifftop between Butcher's & Hunmanby Gaps.

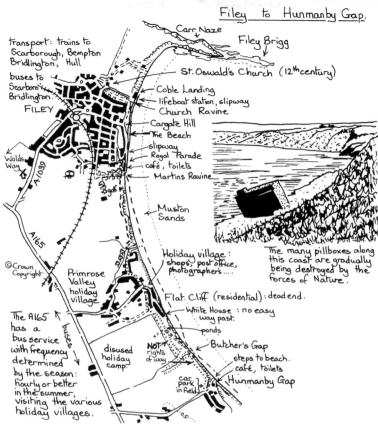

Carr Naze

Filey Brigg

Transport: trains to
Scarborough, Bempton
Bridlington, Hull

buses to
Scarboro',
Bridlington.

FILEY

Wolds
Way

A 1039

St. Oswald's Church (12th century)

Coble Landing

lifeboat station, slipway

Church Ravine

Cargate Hill

The Beach

slipway

Royal Parade

café, toilets

Martins Ravine

golf

Muston
Sands

A165

© Crown
Copyright

Primrose
Valley
holiday
village

Holiday village:
shops, post office,
photographers....

Flat Cliff (residential): dead end.

White House : no easy
way past.

ponds

The A165
has a
bus service
with frequency
determined
by the season:
hourly or better
in the summer,
visiting the various
holiday villages.

buses

disused
holiday
camp.

NOT
rights
of way

Butcher's Gap

steps to beach.
café, toilets

Hunmanby Gap

car park
in field

o.s.

The many pillboxes along
this coast are gradually
being destroyed by the
forces of Nature.

* The clifftop path above the Royal Parade is a delightful way to
reach the cleft of Martin's Ravine. The path continues opposite,
up steps, to follow the clifftop southwards, presently descending
to another gap. From here the best way, tide permitting, is along
the broad sands to Hunmanby Gap (the one with steps and a café!)

If the tide is exceptionally high you may have to wait, or, if
you must, seek an alternative route : you can follow the lane
up into Primrose Valley holiday camp. A path (not dedicated as a right
of way) leaves the south-east corner of the holiday village, and
follows the fence of the old Butlin's camp to Butcher's Gap. Turn
back down to the beach. East of the Gap is another clifftop path.

111.

● The <u>Portacafé</u>, almost on the beach at Hunmanby Gap, is something special. Its mode of construction is at least partly a recognition of this coast's erosion problem. The soft clay cliffs are disappearing at about 0.3 metres per year. When an easterly wind sends the waves crashing up the sandy beach to tear at the overhangs you can see why! Immediately south of the gap (below), the public path has been a victim, and thick gorse inhibits the formation of an alternative. If the sea is lapping at the beach-head, you can retire to the comfort of the tiny cafe (in the right season) and admire the spectacles of Filey Brigg and Bempton Cliffs through the large windows.

Hunmanby Gap.

112.

Hunmanby Gap to Speeton Beach

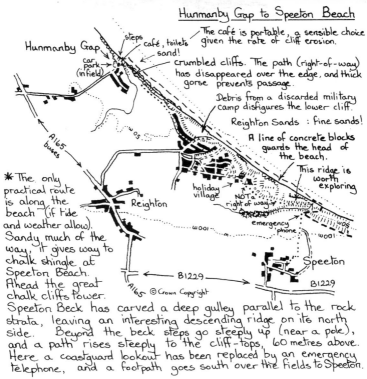

The café is portable, a sensible choice given the rate of cliff erosion.

Hunmanby Gap

steps · café, toilets · sand!

car park (in field)

crumbled cliffs. The path (right-of-way) has disappeared over the edge, and thick gorse prevents passage.

Debris from a discarded military camp disfigures the lower cliff.

Reighton Sands : fine sands!

A line of concrete blocks guards the head of the beach.

This ridge is worth exploring

A165 buses

* The only practical route is along the beach (if tide and weather allow). Sandy much of the way, it gives way to chalk shingle at Speeton Beach. Ahead the great chalk cliffs tower.

Reighton

holiday village

NOT a right of way

emergency phone

Speeton

B1229

A165 © Crown Copyright

B1229

Speeton Beck has carved a deep gulley parallel to the rock strata, leaving an interesting descending ridge on its north side. Beyond the beck steps go steeply up (near a pole), and a path rises steeply to the cliff-tops, 60 metres above. Here a coastguard lookout has been replaced by an emergency telephone, and a footpath goes south over the fields to Speeton.

Speeton Beach

Bempton Cliffs

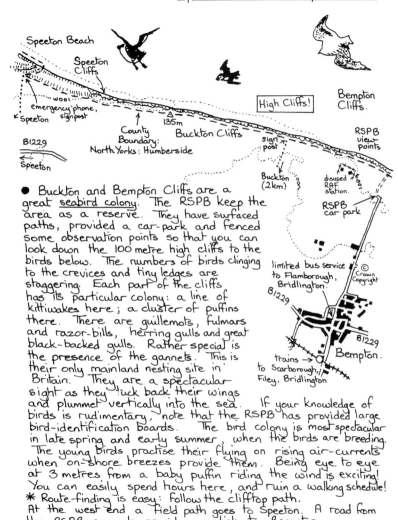

Speeton Beach

Speeton Cliffs

wood

emergency phone, Speeton signpost

High Cliffs!

Bempton Cliffs.

County Boundary: North Yorks: Humberside

135m Buckton Cliffs

sign post

RSPB view points

B1229 Speeton

Buckton (2km)

disused RAF station.

RSPB car park

limited bus service to Flamborough, Bridlington. B1229

© Crown Copyright

B1229 Bempton.

trains → to Scarborough, Filey, Bridlington

● Buckton and Bempton Cliffs are a great <u>seabird colony</u>. The RSPB keep the area as a reserve. They have surfaced paths, provided a car-park and fenced some observation points so that you can look down the 100 metre high cliffs to the birds below. The numbers of birds clinging to the crevices and tiny ledges are staggering. Each part of the cliffs has its particular colony: a line of kittiwakes here; a cluster of puffins there. There are guillemots, fulmars and razor-bills, herring gulls and great black-backed gulls. Rather special is the presence of the gannets. This is their only mainland nesting site in Britain. They are a spectacular sight as they tuck back their wings and plummet vertically into the sea. If your knowledge of birds is rudimentary, note that the RSPB has provided large bird-identification boards. The bird colony is most spectacular in late spring and early summer, when the birds are breeding. The young birds practise their flying on rising air-currents when on-shore breezes provide them. Being eye to eye at 3 metres from a baby puffin riding the wind is exciting! You can easily spend hours here, and ruin a walking schedule! * Route-finding is easy: follow the clifftop path. At the west end a field path goes to Speeton. A road from the RSPB carpark provides a link to Bempton.

115.

- Dane's Dyke, as seen on a map or read about in books, may not excite the imagination. But when you actually see it, the sheer scale of the earthwork is amazing. The Dyke runs for 4km, right across the headland. It exploits a natural drainage gulley on the south side. A huge rampart, 5 metres high, has been thrown up on the east side of the ditch, itself up to 20 metres wide by 6 metres deep, creating a huge defensive barricade. The effort that must have gone into its creation, moving a million or so tonnes of soil and chalk, all with primitive tools, defies description.

It is OLD: far older than the Danish settlements, despite its name. It may be Iron Age (about 0AD, when the Brigantes were the local tribe). But it may be a thousand years older than that, according to evidence from nearby flint tools finds.

The dyke has been colonised by trees for much of its length, providing a rich habitat for wildlife, especially birds. But public access is restricted to the section south of the B1255, where there is a nature trail.

The headland east of the dyke is known as Little Denmark. It has strong historical and dialect links with the Danish settlements in about 800 AD.

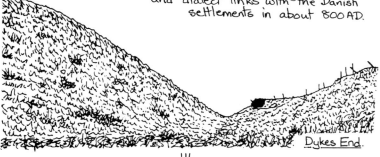

Dykes End.

116.

Bempton Cliffs to North Landing

The cliff top walk east of Bempton Cliffs offers a grand panorama of the Flamborough Headland, as well as intimate views of the cliffs and their inhabitants. The path is waymarked H.W. (Headland Walk).

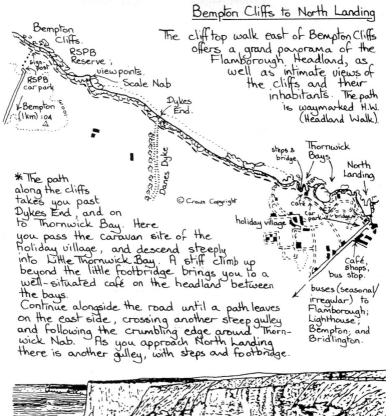

Bempton Cliffs

RSPB Reserve; view points.

sign-post

RSPB car park

← Bempton (1km) 104 △

Scale Nab

Dykes End.

Danes Dyke

© Crown Copyright

steps & bridge

Thornwick Bays

North Landing

café

holiday village

car park

bridge

Café, shops, bus stop.

buses (seasonal / irregular) to Flamborough; Lighthouse; Bempton; and Bridlington.

* The path along the cliffs takes you past Dykes End, and on to Thornwick Bay. Here you pass the caravan site of the holiday village, and descend steeply into Little Thornwick Bay. A stiff climb up beyond the little footbridge brings you to a well-situated café on the headland between the bays.

Continue alongside the road until a path leaves on the east side, crossing another steep gulley and following the crumbling edge around Thornwick Nab. As you approach North Landing there is another gulley, with steps and footbridge.

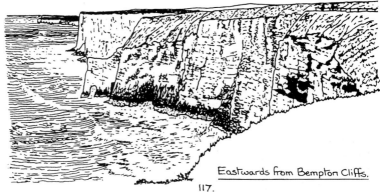

Eastwards from Bempton Cliffs.

Thornwick Bays and North Landing.

North-west from Thornwick Nab, towards Bempton Cliffs.

● The bays at Thornwick and North Landing are real smugglers' coves. Here the chalk has been eroded, leaving headlands honeycombed with sea-level caves, and the tiny bays, each with its sandy floor. Inevitably this combination held great appeal for smugglers, who could take their pick of the many landings around the headland, to the frustration of the Customs officers. They are fascinating places to explore, but take care not to be cut-off by rising tides, and beware strong currents around the headlands.

When the weather is right you may be able to indulge in a boat trip from North Landing to view the bird sanctuary and the caves from the sea. At other times the cobles are drawn well up the steep ramp: a winch-house by the access track provides the hauling-power.

The lifeboat station is at the very top of the beach, with a runway down to the shore or the sea. It is so far above the sea that it is amazing to think of waves reaching its doors. But they did in the 1953 storms. That is the other side of the sea-side life, compared to the idyllic sun-washed cove of turquoise water that you may find in summer.

The clifftops too are another world, of cafés, car-parks, caravans and holiday villages.

North Landing:
the boat ramp; winch
house; lifeboat station.

• Although not in the same league as the Old Man of Hoy, the stacks and cliff scenery around Flamborough Head are impressive. One stack in Selwicks Bay (not this one) is called Eve: a spare rib? (Adam, representing the weaker sex, disappeared years ago).

North Landing to Flamborough Head

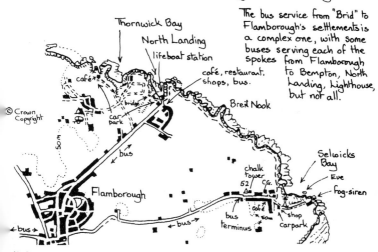

The bus service from "Brid" to Flamborough's settlements is a complex one, with some buses serving each of the spokes from Flamborough to Bempton, North Landing, Lighthouse, but not all.

Labels on map: Thornwick Bay · North Landing · lifeboat station · café, restaurant, shops, bus. · café · bridge · car park · 50m · bus · Flamborough · © Crown Copyright · Breil Nook · chalk tower 52 · C.G. · Selwicks Bay · Eve · fog-siren · café · 50m · shop · carpark · bus terminus · ←bus → · ← bus → · ←bus

* A path leaves beside the café building at the top of the slope at North Landing, and follows the headland edge. It goes fairly uneventfully to Selwicks Bay, dipping and rising like a gentle roller-coaster over the headlands. At Selwicks Bay you climb up to meet the road just west of the lighthouse. This is a tourist outpost, with cafés, shop, carpark......
—make the most of it!

Selwicks Bay

Flamborough Head

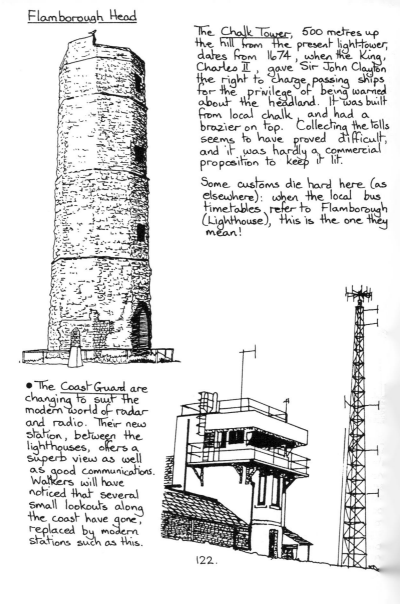

The Chalk Tower, 500 metres up the hill from the present lighttower, dates from 1674, when the King, Charles II, gave Sir John Clayton the right to charge passing ships for the privilege of being warned about the headland. It was built from local chalk, and had a brazier on top. Collecting the tolls seems to have proved difficult, and it was hardly a commercial proposition to keep it lit.

Some customs die hard here (as elsewhere): when the local bus timetables refer to Flamborough (Lighthouse), this is the one they mean!

• The Coast Guard are changing to suit the modern world of radar and radio. Their new station, between the lighthouses, offers a superb view as well as good communications. Walkers will have noticed that several small lookouts along the coast have gone, replaced by modern stations such as this.

122.

Flamborough Head

The modern lighthouse is open to the public on weekday afternoons, from 2pm until 1 hour before dusk.

This light tower was built in 1806, when the Customs Officer in Bridlington, Benjamine Milne, convinced Trinity House that it would reduce the enormous number of wrecks on the headland.
It is 28 metres (92 feet) high, and flashes four times every 15 seconds.

[th]e headland is often shrouded in fog, even when it is sunny [in]land. Then, of course, the lighthouse is rendered useless [an]d the fog signal is [u]sed. The earliest fog [st]ation (1859) used cannon. [r]ockets replaced them [fr]om 1877, followed by [a] pneumatic bull-horn [fr]om 1913. But since 1985 [an] electronically-produced [s]ignal has been used.

Flamborough Head to South Landing.

High Stacks: most easterly point on this coastline.

South Landing

Chalk Tower
coastguard station
fog siren
High Stacks
52√
café
steps down
B 1259
bus terminus
shop, restaurant
Flamborough
© Crown Copyright
Heritage Coast Information Centre
sign-post
South Landing →
picnic tables
stepped gulley
Cliffs!
steps
first (last) view of Bridlington

* From the lighthouse either the broad main track or a variety of minor paths will take you to the Fog Siren. Continue round to the south, along the clifftop past High Stacks Bay. (Explore here if you want to and conditions permit : steps go down to the bay.)
Continue south-westwards along the clifftop.
Descend into South Landing by steps.

South Landing.

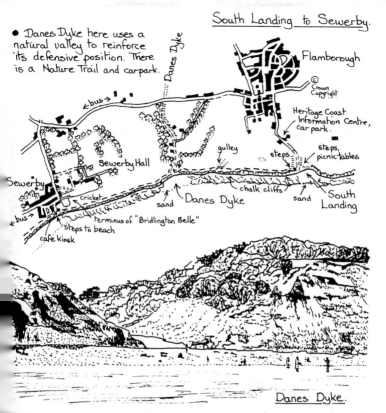

- Danes Dyke here uses a natural valley to reinforce its defensive position. There is a Nature Trail and carpark.

Danes Dyke

Flamborough

© Crown Copyright

Heritage Coast Information Centre, car park.

gulley

steps

steps, picnic tables

Sewerby Hall

chalk cliffs

South Landing

Sewerby

cricket

sand

Danes Dyke

sand

terminus of "Bridlington Belle"

steps to beach

café kiosk

← bus →

Danes Dyke.

• South Landing is another of Flamborough's havens, with its small fleet of cobles. It used to have its own lifeboat too, in the days when muscle-power or sails could not guarantee that the North Landing lifeboat could round the Head in bad weather.

✶ Climb the steps by the old lifeboat house and continue along the clifftop path westwards. The route is interrupted by an odiferous gulley (fortunately with a bridge), then carries on to the steps leading down into the wooded valley of Danes Dyke, and its sandy beach.
A zig-zag path goes up through the edge of the delightful woods to regain the edge of the cliffs for the walk to Sewerby.

127.

Sewerby

Sewerby Hall – the gatehouse.

● The Hall was built in 1714, an elegant house on the
site of the old manor house. It was extended, and in
1811 enclosed in a park, the road from the village being
diverted round the northern boundary. But the land, with
the house, returned to the people when Bridlington bought
it in 1934. Now it is a park and museum, with a
variety of gardens and collections. The monkey-puzzle trees
and yuccas of the Formal Garden are a delight – a hint
of foreign climes – while the Old English Garden, with a
succession of plants in geometrical beds, and the Fragrance
Garden – an aromatic collection – provide lovely complements.
There are interior collections too: an Art Gallery; vintage
motorcycles; Amy Johnson memorabilia; agricultural machines.
Sports too are not forgotten, with greens for Putting,
golf and Crown Green Bowling. Towards the cliffs is
Sewerby Cricket Club: is there a penalty for hitting a six
over the cliffs?

Sewerby

Llamas are not the only
exotic animals to be seen here.
Wallabies and deer also live
in the paddocks. A sunken
lane (Frith Lane) runs between
the enclosures to and from the
village.
Flamingoes and peacock can
be seen too, as well as a
collection of ornamental ducks.

● Not Gulliver in Lilliput.
This is a small part of the model
village at the west end of Sewerby.
It is worth a visit, not just for the
quality of its modelling, but for the humour
it displays.

Sewerby to Bridlington.

A broad beach of sand and chalk pebbles stretches from Sewerby to Bridlington.

As you approach the town there are promenades, with beach chalets, deck chairs, colourful gardens and ice-cream. Residential North Beach gives way to the razamatazz of the harbour area, where the commercial centre of the town overlooks the moorings and the fish quay. This is unashamedly a seaside town, that moves up a gear or two as the holiday season approaches, bringing in the "Westies" from the West Riding.

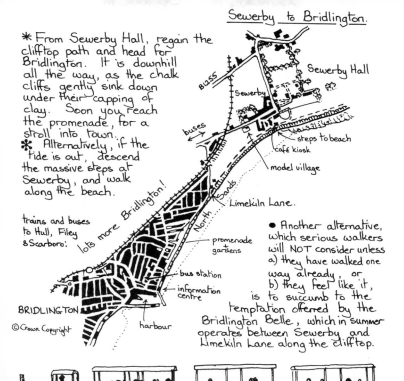

* From Sewerby Hall, regain the clifftop path and head for Bridlington. It is downhill all the way, as the chalk cliffs gently sink down under their capping of clay. Soon you reach the promenade, for a stroll into town.

* Alternatively, if the tide is out, descend the massive steps at Sewerby, and walk along the beach.

* Another alternative, which serious walkers will NOT consider unless a) they have walked one way already, or b) they feel like it, is to succumb to the temptation offered by the Bridlington Belle, which in summer operates between Sewerby and Limekiln Lane along the clifftop.

• Bridlington is the southern terminus of this book. The traditional Yorkshire coastline (now in Humberside) goes on, of course, for another 60km or so, until it terminates abruptly at Spurn Head. But that is an altogether different coastline from the varied line of rugged cliffs that have stretched south from Saltburn: south of here broad sands backed by low bluffs of clay are the norm. Of course, if you have the energy and the inclination, keep on walking!

Bridlington

Bridlington harbour is still an active commercial fishing port, with its own fleet and facilities for visitors and their catches.

It also provides moorings for many yachts and other pleasure craft, plus the necessary lifeboat.

Perhaps of most interest to the explorer who has arrived on foot are the large launches that offer trips to see Flamborough Head from the sea. Give your feet a rest — take a boat trip!

Bibliography:

These books have been helpful, informative, entertaining, and may interest you also. The list is not in any particular order, of merit, topic, nor anything else.

'The Cleveland Way'   A. Falconer   HMSO, 1972
'Portrait of Yorkshire'   H. Scott,   Robert Hale, 1965
'Rambler's Riding'   A. Falconer
'A Guide to the Cleveland Way' M. Boyes, Constable, 1977
'A Guide to the Cleveland Way' R. Sale,   Constable, 1987
'North York Moors National Park'   HMSO, 1969
'The Face of North-East Yorkshire' Eyre & Palmer, Dalesman, 1973
'Robin Hood's Bay'   E. Gower   Dalesman. 1986
'Geology of the Yorkshire Coast', Hemingway et al., Geologist Assoc. 1968
'British Mesozoic Fossils'   British Museum, 1975
'Whitby'   E. Gower   Dalesman 1985
'Yorkshire Coast'   Dalesman 1984
'Cleveland Industrial Heritage' Scarborough. B.C. Community
                                             Programme Agency, 1989
'Scarborough Castle'   HMSO / English Heritage, 1988
'The History of Saltburn'   C.S. Wilson   Seaside Books, 1983
'Saltburn Times'   C.S. Wilson   Seaside Books, 1987
'Memories of Marske'   P. Sotheran   A.A. Sotheran, 1976
'Ordnance Survey Leisure Guide: North York Moors' AA/OS 1987
'Cleveland Way Companion' P. Hannon   Hillside, 1986
'Walks on the N.Y. Moors, Book 3' P. Hannon   Hillside, 1988
'Birdwatcher's Britain' ed: J. Parslow,   Pan / O.S. 1983
'Walks for Motorists, N.Y. Moors, N.S.E.', G. White, Fredk. Warne 1974
'Walking on the North York Moors', Ramblers Assocⁿ., Dalesman, 1973
'A. Walker on the Cleveland Way', C. Walker, Pendyke, 1977
'Ancient Cleveland from the Air' R. Crosthwaite, Tees Towing, 1987
'Railways of Teesside'   K. Hoole.   Dalesman 1982
'The Scarborough & Whitby Railway' J.R. Lidster, Hendon 1977
'North-Eastern Branch Lines since 1925', K. Hoole Ian Allan 1978
'Frank Meadow Sutcliffe, Photographer' 1 & 2, Sutcliffe Gallery.
'The Story of Whitby's Old Parish Church', G. Austen   1954
'Ravenscar Geological Trail'   N.Y.M. Nat. Park
'Sandsend Trail'   N.Y.M. Nat. Park
'Monasteries of North-East Yorkshire'   HMSO 1962.
'Coastal Walks of England and Wales' C. Somerville, Grafton, 1988

The North York Moors National Park have published a wide range of informative leaflets in a 'Heritage Coast' series, covering such topics as 'Fishing Boats', 'Seabirds', 'Fossils', 'Mining and Quarrying', 'Runswick Bay', 'Robin Hood's Bay' .....

Index:

Symbols used on the sketch maps

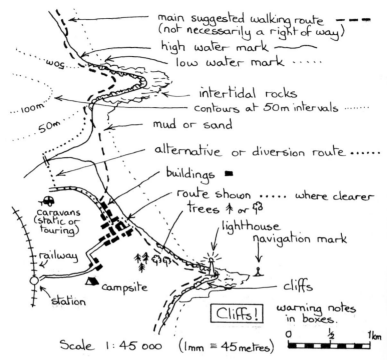

main suggested walking route – – –
(not necessarily a right of way)

high water mark ⌣

low water mark · · · · ·

intertidal rocks

contours at 50m intervals ·······

mud or sand

alternative or diversion route ······

buildings ■

route shown ····· where clearer

trees ♠ or ♣

lighthouse

navigation mark

caravans (static or touring)

railway

station

campsite

cliffs

Cliffs!   warning notes in boxes.

wos

100m

50m

Scale 1 : 45 000   (1mm ≡ 45 metres)

0   ½   1 km

The routes shown are not necessarily rights of way.
There are some permissive paths (ie paths where you
have permission to WALK!) and some rights of way.
South of Filey there are places where the status of paths
is unclear.
For specific information use the Ordnance Survey maps.

Remember too that the coast constantly changes. Cliffs
in particular are prone to erosion, so that paths slip
away between one year and the next. Some have
been reinforced, some replaced – and some have lapsed.
Agreements between landowners and the County Highways
people also result in diversions, closures or creations
of paths.